or Cow Barn
Bought at Burkholders
"Used Books"

Agnes Mishler

Call It Zest

Among the books by ELIZABETH YATES
The Road through Sandwich Notch
The Lady from Vermont
A Book of Hours
The Lighted Heart
Up the Golden Stair
On That Night
Skeezer, Dog with a Mission
Is There a Doctor in the Barn?
Howard Thurman, Portrait of a Practical Dreamer
The Next Fine Day
Your Prayers and Mine
Nearby

For Young People
Amos Fortune, Free Man (Newbery Medal winner)
Prudence Crandall, Woman of Courage
Patterns on the Wall
Mountain Born
A Place for Peter
We, the People
Carolina's Courage
Sarah Whitcher's Story
Someday You'll Write

Call It Zest

The Vital Ingredient After Seventy

ELIZABETH YATES

The Stephen Greene Press

Brattleboro, Vermont

The author is grateful to the following for permission to quote this material:

to Elizabeth Gray Vining for the prayer quoted on pages 89 and 90; to Macmillan Publishing Company for "Now in the Stillness" from *Down Half the World* by Elizabeth Coatsworth (Copyright © 1968 by Elizabeth Coatsworth Beston);

to Yankee, Inc., for "Body and Spirit" by Elizabeth Coatsworth, reprinted with permission from the March 1957 issue of Yankee Magazine, published by Yankee, Inc., Dublin, N.H.

Copyright © 1977 by Elizabeth Yates McGreal

All rights reserved. No part of this book may be reproduced without written permission from the publisher, except by a reviewer who may quote brief passages or reproduce illustrations in a review; nor may any part of this book be reproduced, stored in a retrieval system, or transmitted in any form or by any means electronic, mechanical, photocopying, recording, or other, without written permission from the publisher.

This book has been produced in the United States of America. It is designed by R. L. Dothard Associates and is published by The Stephen Greene Press, Brattleboro, Vermont 05301

LIBRARY OF CONGRESS CATALOGING IN PUBLICATION DATA
Yates, Elizabeth, 1905–
Call it zest.
1. Aged—Conduct of life. I. Title.
BJ1691.Y37   170'.202'26   76-50270
ISBN 0-8289-0296-8

Contents

PROLOGUE   ix
DEDICATION   xi
Birthday Celebration   1
    Clara Sipprell and Phyllis Fenner
"To Return to Oneself"   12
    Elizabeth Coatsworth
"Not for Sissies"   21
    Margaret Henrichsen
Head Into the Wind   32
    Allen W. Clark
Five Apples a Day   44
    Dan Barry
"I Make a Little Joke"   53
    Anna Yoss
Awake the Dawn   60
    Eve Dawson
A Cheerful Heart Is a Good Medicine   72
    Edwin C. Miller, M.D.
"And All Shall Be Well"   83
    Elizabeth Gray Vining
To Make a Plan   94
    Lloyd P. Young

A Man with Roots   103
    Henry Ziba Persons
Melody of a Life   119
    Frances Mann
"I Make Easy Friends"   129
    Ernest F. Kroner
"You Don't Think I'm Going to Sit Down, Do You?"   140
    Isabelle Andrews Buchanan
"I Want to Help"   151
    Edward S. Boote
The Balanced Equation   165
    Robert C. Charman, M.D.
THAT MOUNTAIN: AN EPILOGUE   171
AUTHOR'S NOTE   176

Prologue

*What has happened? It is life
that has happened, and I am old.*
—Louis Aragon

Who said it to me, or where, I can't recall, but that is unimportant. The question was, "How old are you?" And when I replied "Sixty," there was silence. Shock seemed to vibrate on the air as if I had said or done something wrong. Then came the response, "I can't believe it!"

That was ten years ago, ten years during which there have been occasional pert reminders. Like the time I met an acquaintance in the post office and told her about my new dog. "You mean you've got a puppy at your——" Then she caught herself and smiled politely.

Or the day the young couple thought I looked tired and offered to do my shopping "or any errands you may have, to save you." My inner resistance rose like mercury in the sun until I told myself that they must really care about me, and that was enough to make one grateful; for love is rare and any evidence of it is to be cherished.

Then the other day I exclaimed to a friend that I was finding it fascinating to get up the ladder of years, there were so many discoveries —but I never had a chance to say what they were because she interrupted me: "You mean you really like getting old?"

"Yes."

She didn't give me a chance to tell her why.

Dedicated to the people in this book,

for it is they who made it:

I asked them questions

and listened to

their answers.

Birthday Celebration

PHYLLIS FENNER
CLARA SIPPRELL

*I*t was a cold night in early November, not raining, not snowing, but with a hint that either or both might happen by morning. Winter was on the way. We were ready for it, even looked forward to it. The fire was lively on the hearth, a casserole was in the oven. Phyllis and Clara had driven over from Vermont to celebrate their joint birthdays: two weeks apart on the calendar, fourteen years otherwise.

The cake was made and iced. I couldn't cope with a galaxy of candles so had settled for two. Wished and blown upon with two deep-drawn breaths, it was fairly certain that the flames would be extinguished and the wishes come true, each one making it possible for the other as they had been doing for a good many years. The number of candles didn't matter any more than the number of years attained mattered. A birthday was not so much an occasion to count time as a cause for celebration.

Phyllis, standing by the fire, exclaimed for the

third time, "I just think it's funny to be seventy years old!"

I think I knew what she meant: to feel no different in the inmost self than one did at any other age when aware of a place in the world and work to do, and yet also to know that something subtle has happened and one is not the same. One is wiser and there is less time for accomplishment.

Firelight flickered on the sherry I had just poured into the Waterford glasses, turning amber to gold. I lifted mine and held it toward Phyllis. "Happiness! Ever—whatever."

Clara made one of her murmuring sounds indicative of pleasure that knew no words.

"I've always been happy," Phyllis began, "without being conscious of happiness as such. Maybe it's because when I was a little girl I felt secure. I knew I was loved."

"Tell us," for though I had known Phyllis as a writer and as a librarian for a good half of those seventy years that amused her so, I knew very little about her early life.

Phyllis stood with her back to the fire, a sturdy compact figure in well-tailored slacks, her dark blue shirt setting off a silver chain with a round pendant that spoke of some far part of the world. Her short brown hair was scarcely touched with gray, her rimmed glasses accentuated the roundness of her face. The fire, the day, and just her own good health had given color to her cheeks. By contrast her lips seemed pale, but Phyllis had no use for lipstick. I'd heard her say once that she'd feel a phony if she ever used make-up.

"My father had the family general store in Almond, New York," she began, "and I don't suppose we ever had much money, but we never thought about it and we never wanted beyond what we had. As a child I had a playhouse made from the top of a grocery wagon. It was bright yellow and said on it A. J. FENNER & SONS— BOOTS, SHOES, HARDWARE, GROCERIES, ETC. Wasn't that fun? My father did his same work until somewhere in his seventies and died in his eighties. He took things slowly, thought a lot, and didn't say much. But when someone asked him what he'd do if he had just a day to live, he said he'd spend it churning butter, for time passes slowly when you churn. He was good without being good, don't you know."

"Open that up a little, Phyllis," Clara said.

"Well, we weren't regular churchgoers like lots of people, just sort of casual."

"But you pray."

"Sure, but not on my knees. Every life has a plan, but if things get too organized you may feel you lose your place in that plan."

"And your mother?"

Phyllis made me see her mother reading from *Grimm's Fairy Tales*, then making up stories for the wide-eyed little girl who could have listened all night. Cruel things happened in the stories, often bad things, but they only made the little girl feel how secure she was, how loved. "Listening to her gave me my place in the sun." There was a phonograph in the store. "It had a big horn like a morning-glory and a stack of records beside it. Mother wouldn't tolerate it in the house but once a year she let me borrow it for a whole day, with all the records I wanted. Then back to the store it went.

"When I was old enough to have a bicycle, Mother told me I could go wherever I wanted to. 'Your judgment is as good as mine,' she said. I wore little overalls which she made for me and when someone once asked me what I'd do if I were ever asked to the White House, 'I'd just be myself,' I said. You can't live if you can't be natural, don't you know. Convention leaves me cold."

Her glass no longer flickered with golden light so I refilled it. "And then?"

After graduation from Mount Holyoke College, it was a question of finding herself and her work. She tried many jobs—a department store, teaching, library work followed by a year at Columbia Library school, then the way was clear. For thirty-two years she was a children's librarian, doing for others what her mother had done for her. In 1941 the first of her more than forty books was published. "As a family we'd never been concerned about money, but as the years moved along and brought their problems, it was good to have a little extra from the books to help out."

"You never wanted to marry?"

"I was engaged twice, but a friend said to me, 'If you stay unmarried till you're fifty you'll be glad.' And I am." She paused and turned to look into the fire. "I guess you'd say that I never had any reason to doubt about love, and I've spent no time or energy in regrets. I've done a lot of enjoying," she turned back to us again, "and now I'm seventy."

As if on cue, my timer sounded from the kitchen. I was in no hurry to answer it. A casserole can always take another few minutes.

"Her master's voice," Phyllis said.

With that reminder, I left to put the meal on the table.

It was not until after dinner that we got back to the subject of time.

"I guess I'll get used to it," Phyllis remarked. "Maybe someday it won't even seem funny."

"What?"

"Being seventy."

"I don't care how old I am," Clara murmured dreamily. "I just know I've had a delicious dinner that ended with a piece of birthday cake."

"You're eighty-four," Phyllis said, a trace of the school teacher in her voice.

"Oh?" Clara's tone was surprised. "Does it matter?"

Looking at her, one would think it had mattered very little. Her dark brown hair only

BIRTHDAY CELEBRATION 5

streaked with gray was done in long braids coiled around her head like a crown; her brown eyes had the warmth of her heart in them; her skin was firm and smooth, creased only near the mouth that smiled through her words and near her eyes that squinted behind a camera. She dressed most frequently in browns and grays, with peasant embroidery to her blouses and heavy antique jewelry, each piece with a story to tell. She wore capes with a flair; they wrapped her up against cold or wind or rain, and watching her unfurl herself from one gave the feeling that, if need be, she could as easily enclose another in their spaciousness as in her heart. This night she wore a smoke-gray dress and a chain of silver links which she fingered frequently. Clara, the photographer, was different from Phyllis, the writer, yet each one was a natural.

"Oh," she said, picking up an earlier thread of conversation, "you had your father, Phyllis, you had him all the time you were growing up, and mine died before I was born, but I felt his presence. I never wondered what I would do when I grew up because I was doing it all the time I was growing, and skipping my way through school."

"Photography?" I asked.

She nodded. "I worked in my brother's studio, doing whatever he gave me to do, and dreaming of the day when I would have my own studio.

There was never much money, but something better: faith. When we needed money for rent or food, it always came, it always has come. And I loved to go to church, more for the hymn-singing than anything else. But I never sang, I shouted! Especially that one 'Just as I Am.'" Clara hummed it gaily, tapping one foot on the floor and bringing her finger tips together in silent beating.

Her mood changed. "I was sixteen when I discovered poetry—Keats, Browning, Emerson, then Sidney Lanier. His words are still like a golden strand in my memory. Lanier and my mother's opal ring brought me into the heart of beauty, making me aware of texture and color. I know I was sixteen, because that was the year I started to make pictures, still for my brother, not yet for myself; but I knew what I had been born to do. My work and my goal were the same. Oh, there was hardship as the years went on. We were poor, even miserable sometimes, but sittings began to come my way and skill grew. There were people who helped me, and there was travel." She laughed, the lightest ripple of sound. *"Want big* were my key words."

Clara soon moved from her brother's studio to her own in New York City; she moved from doing familiar people to the famous; but always she found as much pleasure in doing a Vermont farmer in his field as the King of Sweden in his palace. With her camera she was never shy, and she never found herself in a place where she did not belong. She worked only with natural light. On a slightly clouded day or even one of falling mist, invariably this gave better results than full sunshine, unless she needed sun for shadow in her picture. Once, when doing Albert Einstein, she set her camera up and started to pitch the large black cloth over it and her head. When he asked, "Are you going in there?" She replied, "Yes." They understood each other.

Prepared well in advance for a sitting, Clara had an unhurried way that put her subject at ease. With time to spend quietly, she often turned over in her mind words she cherished:

> *The Light of God surrounds thee,*
> *The Love of God enfolds thee,*
> *The Power of God protects thee,*
> *The Presence of God watches over thee.*

Constantly she found men easier to do than women. Often what came through on the plate was telltale—a lack of satisfaction, a lack of security, for there were many people trying to be what they were not. Conversely, a strong life that knew fulfillment accentuated good features. People sometimes looked older in their pictures, more mature or dignified or distinguished, than they thought themselves to be. When they seemed surprised, Clara told them they would look like that in another five years. She did not attempt to please but to see true, and the camera could often be trusted more than the eye.

"Have you ever made a perfect picture?" I asked.

Her brown eyes widened as her glance met mine. Her smile seemed to belie the slow shaking of her head. "I almost would not want to, there'd be nothing more to aim for."

Because she was deeply satisfied in doing work she loved, she was sensitive of people for whom life had little tranquillity. "They struggle too hard instead of living within their scope, they don't go with the flow of time; and so many are lonely. I've been alone much of my life, but never lonely. I'm—" she searched for a word that would best describe herself—"replete!" she announced.

"You held to your dream," I reminded her, thinking of the opal, and poetry, and being sixteen.

"To relinquish it would have been sin, perhaps the only sin. No—" she caught herself quickly, "there's a Tibetan saying that I like: 'The only sin is to live in outworn patterns.'"

The mention of Tibet recalled to me that they would soon be leaving for several months in Europe, Jugoslavia this time, ending up with a few weeks in Florence. Clara spoke eagerly about the weeks ahead.

"I like to press my feet on another soil, feel

the atmosphere, see the people. Museums and galleries and churches are right for the life that has been, but the life that is being lived today is the one I want to have part in."

"And make pictures?"

"Oh, yes!"

"Do you mind being in your mid-eighties?"

"No! I'm crazy about it. To resent is lack of acceptance. I've never been so happy as I am now, nor so rich."

"She's never owed anyone a nickel," Phyllis put in, "never had a debt in her life. That's why she's so rich."

Clara moved her hand across her face with an air of mystery which Phyllis dispelled.

"She sleeps everything off," Phyllis added. "If it's a cold or a pain in her heart she goes to bed and sleeps; and if something happens that makes her mad, don't you know, she gets sick. Then she has to go to bed."

Remembering Phyllis's remark about her father, I turned it on Clara. "If you had a year to live, or even a day, what would you do?"

"Not a damned thing different."

* * *

At the time I did not realize that the conversation on that November evening would be the beginning of a round. Conversation has a way of continuing in the mind and I found myself thinking of people I knew well, and others of whom I had heard. Time had taken each one by the hand, for no one who came into my mind was less than seventy but all were still contributing to life. Wondering about them made me want to seek them out.

I felt sure that none of them had been obsessed by either of the two drives: to gain wealth, to achieve fame; but that each one at some time had discovered life's particular gift and sought to develop it, then keep it in use. I guessed that an inner resilience had become a spiritual flexibility.

Perhaps as I talked with them I would find out that "the pursuit of happiness" and a spirit of usefulness had very little to do with the accident of birth or the advantages of education, but a very great deal to do with an early environment of love and a conviction that there is always something ahead. Pablo Casals, the cellist, gave a hint of this when, at the age of ninety, he was asked why he still practiced so many hours a day. "Because I think I am improving," he replied. Edwin Muir, the English poet, indicated it in his poem "The Way," especially in its concluding lines:

And what will come at last?
The way leads on.

"To Return to Oneself"

ELIZABETH COATSWORTH

*M*y first meeting with Elizabeth Coatsworth was in 1923 in her newly published book of poems, *Fox Footprints*. And, because she had crossed her threshold as a writer and I was a very long way from even approaching mine, I handled the pages with awe and found myself repeating phrases with reverence. This was the marvel of the span made by the word: treasures of her mind had now become jewels in mine.

Through the years we met occasionally. I cherished her books and those of her husband, Henry Beston; and I knew that their achievements were many, one of them being a richly happy marriage that shone out on a troubled world like a lighthouse on the coast—the Maine coast which they both knew well and had written about in their separate ways. And I had crossed the threshold of her home on other occasions.

As I was to be in Maine and not far from her on September fourth and fifth, I wrote to ask if I might come by on one of those days for an hour's visit. She telephoned me as soon as she received my letter and said with a cheery briskness, "The first idea is always the best. Come on the fourth."

"About three o'clock?"

"Good!" she exclaimed, "for I do like to have my nap after luncheon."

It was warm and pleasantly windy when I followed the familiar road out from the village of Nobleboro. Clouds piled up against clouds, then scattered across the blue; their changing shapes made shifting shadows on the brilliantly green fields that sloped down to the waters of Damariscotta Pond. At the end of the road was the low-built red house, Chimney Farm. It looked snug, fitted to the land, and welcoming. A bird's swift passage drew my eyes up to the edge of the woods and the stones of a small family cemetery. One of them was Henry Beston's. When I looked back, Elizabeth Coatsworth stood in the doorway to greet me, tall and straight, with an air that was at the same time commanding and warm.

A neighbor who had come in earlier to visit was just leaving. Somewhere in the house there were sounds that said a piano was being tuned. Tamar, the big black poodle, sniffed me thoroughly then nudged against her mistress as if to assure her that it was all right for me to be there. Then we went inside, out of the windy sunshine and into another kind of light.

Rooms in old New England farmhouses are

generally small and low-ceilinged, the better to hold heat in winter. At Chimney Farm every room had shelves of books, reminders of the family in pictures, of travel in charming mementos. In the little room near the doorway where we sat everything spoke comfort—the chairs, the sun pouring in, the Franklin stove ready to mitigate cold; and everything spoke a particular kind of caring. There were treasures from the Orient, Eskimo carvings, paintings, unusual books. I felt embraced by beauty, and I had the feeling that each lovely thing had a story to tell.

Elizabeth left me for a moment to go to the kitchen. Intriguing sounds could soon be heard, then she returned with a great pitcher of iced tea, a plate of cakes that Tamar observed longingly, and four ice-filled glasses. It was always well to be ready at that time of day for other callers. If I was being observant, she was no less so. Handing me a tall glass of the tea, she commented on the way a carnelian stone in my necklace "so perfectly" matched my sweater.

Then we talked. How we talked! First about books and soon, rather especially, about those each one of us was currently involved in writing.

"I'm alive," she said, as vibrantly as if greeting the challenge of a new day, "and writing is the core of my being."

Again she left me, walking with a certain deliberation, to return with a book.

"There's something wonderful about a new

book. It's like handling a newborn baby. This won't be out for another month, but I'd like you to have a copy now." She found a pen and wrote in it to me, *With my love,* then signed it with her quick casual signature.

I hugged it to my heart and thought how truly wonderful it was to be given such a gift, at such a time, on such a day.

I told her that I treasured her last book of poems, *Down Half the World,* and that there was one I liked so much that I had copied it into my notebook.

"You have it with you?"

"Yes."

"Then read it to me."

So I read to her "Body and Spirit":

"The body keeps an accurate account of years.
They are like fagots, laid upon its back,
which it must carry down a darkening road
to an unlighted house.
But the bold spirit
pays little heed to time. If it grow weary
it is through sorrow, not through age. It looks
daily upon its image in the glass
with a surprised contempt. What is this
   creature?
This is a glove that does not fit my hand."

She leaned forward to listen. I was aware of her expression: intent, interested, almost as if the words were new to her. But perhaps what was new was my feeling for them and the way they had spoken to me. A writer never gets the acclaim that a musician does—immediate applause, often encouraging an encore. Her words, in another's voice, might have given an acclaim that was heartening.

"The poem in that book that young people like is 'Now in the Stillness,' " she said, and then she said it to me.

> "*Now in the stillness and the aloneness*
> *the blossom returns to the tree,*
> *and the bird to its nest,*
>
> *the light returns to the water,*
> *the shadow to the boulder,*
> *and I return to myself.*"

From somewhere in the house I heard a clock strike the half-hour and everything in me longed for time to stand still.

"That is the real joy of these present years," she went on, "the quietude that comes to one when we move into the deepest realities of life. The different decades have all been appropriate in their ways. I found that the seventies were the time for getting things done, and now the eighties are like the bird and the light and the shadow—a time to return to oneself. Decisions don't have to be made any more, for they are made by circumstances. And death . . ." she paused, holding the word tenderly. The sound, as she said it, was that of a bell being lightly struck. "Who was it said that to think of it was like looking at the sun, it can't be done for long. Do you remember Yeats's poem about the Chinese, the old, old men in a rendezvous on a high mountain, drinking wine together and looking out over a vast plain which might have been their lives—'their eyes, their glittering eyes, are gay.'"

"You said," I reminded her, "in your preface to *The Sparrow Bush* that poetry is the voice of the heart."

"It is."

"And that poetry has the power of prophecy."

Her eyes and mine met. It was a moment of felicity for which no words were needed.

The cheerful but oddly insistent sounds of the piano being tuned had ceased. Footsteps could be heard crossing the floor, then the tuner stood in the doorway. He looked, with his little black bag, like a doctor making a house call.

"I hope you'll have a nice winter," he said, and smiled as he left.

"Winter!" she echoed, and there was excitement in her tone. "The best time for work, and for reading."

I knew she didn't go away. Travel had been a delightful part of her life once, but now the days at Chimney Farm, the weeks, and even the long winter months, were deep in content. The pattern she has achieved is an enviable one. A neighbor comes in during the late afternoon to prepare supper and spend the night. Tamar, youthfully jaunty at three but quite aware of her responsibility, is a reliable house companion. One or another of the two daughters or the eight grandchildren come on visits, and friends find her out as I had on this September day that still had summer in its warm windiness.

"You know, I've come to like reading detective stories," she said, "they're so well crafted. They have a beginning, a middle, an end, and a plot that carries from the first lines to the last. Reading gives me pleasure, second only to writing, but there's much in contemporary fiction that once read I want to spew out of my mind."

The accent she put on *spew* made us both laugh.

She left the room in search of something and came back with a little pocket sketchbook which she had had with her on one of her first visits to Paris and London when she was a young girl. The sketches were charming, fragile, with touches of humor; the colors were tertiary and soft.

"A young person sees everything so intensely, as if it were the only time, the only one of its kind," she said. "That's the way I saw things then and, with more than half a century between, that's the way I see things now."

She took the book back when I had turned its

last page, then held it as if it were a lovable curiosity. "But I had to decide whether I would be a fourth-rate artist, or a writer. I've never regretted my decision."

Looking at her, it was not Elizabeth Coatsworth I saw but one of her characters, Margaret Winslow in *Here I Stay*. A book read many times, it is my favorite of all her books. Margaret Winslow, too, had to make a hard decision. As she did, she found her own way and with it a completeness that had no dependence on others. She was free and strong in spirit when John Grant entered her life; and with what riches. Dedications in books sometimes have profound meaning. Elizabeth Coatsworth dedicated *Here I Stay* "With love to Henry, this book in which he will often find the far-off mirror of his thought."

When I left her it was with the feeling that she who had written many books and taken joy in the writing of poetry, was being poetry.

The resonant tone of her voice came back to me that night as I read the book she had given me, relishing its economy of phrase and its grace. Reading, I heard her voice, speaking slowly, enunciating words carefully. It was the way a a writer who knows the value of words would speak.

Later, much later, when I had put out my light, I lay listening to the slow surge of the incoming tide with its muted thunder as it crashed against rocks; I watched the distant winking of the beam from a lighthouse; and I breathed with ecstasy the sea air coming in my window. Going back over Elizabeth Coatsworth's books and her life, each a part of the other, I thought how clearly her feeling for the land came through, for its people and the stories that were the fabric of their lives. Some of them were of everyday happenings; others had to do with the mysterious world that exists not on the other side of time but the other side of the ordinary.

At home herself, with roots deep in land she loves, she gave me a feeling of vivid hospitality; not only to me as a tea-time guest, but to ideas, to life, to each new day. Putting the light on again, I read the final paragraph of her book *Maine Memories* which I had brought along with me:

. . . If Americans are to become really at home in America it must be through the devotion of many people to many small deeply loved places. The field by the sea, the single mountain peak seen from a man's door, the island of trees and farm buildings in the western wheat, must be sung and painted and praised until each takes on the gentleness of the thing long loved, and becomes an unconscious part of us and we of it.

The sea swelled in and out with the tide. The light flashed intermittently. The night spelled content.

"Not for Sissies"

MARGARET HENRICHSEN

*H*ow exactly right, I thought, as I came over the road from Ellsworth, Maine, to North Sullivan, to see before me one slender white steeple rising out of and above the leafy green of the trees and towering far above the pointed tips of the firs. My first acquaintance with Dr. Henrichsen had been through her book *Seven Steeples,* the story of her experiences as a minister with seven small churches in her charge. Later I had heard her lecture, and soon after that an exchange of letters made us friends.

It was a day of mist and fog and frequent rain. The land had a sodden look, and where the sea rolled in the rocks were as wet from fresh water as from salt. To my inland eyes, the beauty was such that it made me want to drink it deep into my being. Near things looked far, and shifting mist made far things look near. Like a view of time and space, I thought, fusing together so the two become one.

Margaret stood in her doorway to greet me,

quite filling it; then she led me down the short length of hall to the kitchen. Her steps were carefully made, for she had come out of an accident a while ago with legs not so reliable as once they had been. Taking a pan of blueberry muffins from the oven, she asked me to put them on a plate; then she brought from the stove something that only a Maine-coast kitchen could produce—a crabflake pancake.

We sat down at the small table near the window. Warmth from the stove filled the room and took away all dampness from the day. In my mind were words of hers from her book, words she had used at weddings but to me they seemed right for this moment when two friends had met together, "May the grace of God be in your eyes and on your lips, be in your hands and in your heart."

She asked me about myself, and just being in her presence gave me the feeling that I could tell her anything, my sins and sorrows as well as my joys. But I so relished listening to the rich tone of her voice with its frequent spirited laughter that I had no desire to talk about myself.

"I like being seventy-five," she exclaimed, "but I will say that aging is not for sissies."

"That's the title of a book, taken from a remark of Douglas Steere's."

She had not known of the book so I said I would send her a copy when I got home.

No longer is her ministry that of seven steeples, but of one, and only during the summer months. Scripture reading and pastoral prayer are given seated; she stands for her sermon. She told me that she had, at last and not without a struggle, made up her mind to go into a retirement home near Boston during the winter months.

"Being here and as I am now, I have to depend on my neighbors too much, and that is not right. But I'll come back to this house that I have loved for so long, to my friends in these villages, and to take the service at Sorrento during the summer. One never retires from the ministry."

I asked her what she would do, for it was hard to think of her away from Maine and the country folk to whom she had meant so much and who meant equally much to her.

"I shall write another book; it's been in my mind for a long time. I'll keep myself available for people. And I'll read."

It was as simple and direct and definite as that.

My thoughts went back to the first pages of her *Seven Steeples*. After the death of her husband she had faced the challenge "to be useful, to make a new life surroundings—find meaning in years that stretched so emptily ahead." A career in social work had given her a feeling for people. Ministering to them in one way, she began to see that she might minister in a deeper way. A series of inspired events happened, which within the year brought her to Maine and into the service of several small churches, long without a pastor. Good sense, physical sturdiness, lively humor, innate simplicity were all hers, and they were in the Maine people, too. From the first she felt that she was where she belonged. The education necessary for her ordination came as she studied and met the requirements; the education of the heart came as she preached and visited, married and christened, buried and comforted the people of the churches in her care.

The decision she had come to now after more than thirty gloriously useful years was made in the light of continuing usefulness.

"Our prayers are answered in ways beyond our planning," she said as if in summation.

We talked of prayer. To me it was becoming more and more an opening of the self to God.

"Yes," she said, "and with that opening an increasing sensitivity that readies us to respond to the leading, to the need, God's ways of getting through to us."

The telephone rang and while she attended to it I was glad for the space in our spoken words that gave me time to think about what we had been saying.

We were still sitting at the table when a knock came at the door. It was a young minister and his wife journeying through Maine. They had read about her and wanted to meet her. She took them into her study, a small room just off the kitchen. While they were visiting I did the dishes and had time to go on thinking. When school was out, a troop of children came by her house, bobbing under their yellow fishermen's hats and bright slickers like a flowerbed on the march. They stopped long enough to tap on the glass and peer in, but realizing she had visitors they went on their way.

When the two young people left, I joined her in the study. Small as the room was, it held the nurture and outreach of her life. Her chair was large and comfortable. Before her on the desk was her typewriter, a telephone, a small television set. There were piles of books with markers in them, and letters that looked as if they were waiting to be answered. At her left was a table in front of a window with books and magazines, beside them a small folding clock that seemed there merely to inform and not in any way to dominate. Behind her was a larger table with newspapers and more books. A barometer hung near the doorway. From a basket on the floor flowed her needlework, some crewel embroidery. "Sometimes it's better than reading," she said.

Another telephone call gave me a chance to study the books in a shelf on the wall behind her. There wasn't one that I didn't want to read, or perhaps had read.

Leading off from the study was a glassed-in

porch that must be filled with sunshine on bright days, for there were geraniums, impatiens and other plants giving color and bloom. At the right of her big chair was a space with a straight chair for me, or anyone who might come in to talk with her. I marveled that all which meant most to her —work, communication with others, relaxation, the world by way of air waves—was within easy reach. Here was the compass for her mind, the wellspring for her spirit. I would have liked to straighten things up a bit, but I had the feeling that she knew where everything was, and so it proved. More than once during our conversation she wanted to show me something from among the papers on her desk. Without searching or fumbling, she put her fingers on what was needed and handed it to me.

We spoke of the books we were reading.

"Do you know Frederick Buechner's *Wishful Thinking*?" she asked.

When I shook my head, she got up from her deep chair with the ease of movement often possessed by a large person whose mind is winged, and went to a bookcase. "Here's something I particularly like," she said, "it's on page twelve." Then she read aloud, " 'When I tell somebody my name, I have given him a hold over me that he didn't have before . . . In the book of Exodus, God tells Moses that his name is Yahweh, and God hasn't had a peaceful minute since.' "

I told her of the Anker Larsen book, *With the Door Open,* that I was reading. It was new to her. I wanted to share with her the story of the old peasant who, when he was dying, asked his son to promise to sit every day for one half-hour alone in the best room in the house. The son did, and became a man whom the whole district admired and turned to.

She nodded, then repeated in a charmed tone, "The best room."

"It wouldn't always be the same room, would it?" I asked.

"Of course not: the best at that particular time and for that particular need."

She spoke of her grandfather, an itinerant preacher, "but a Moses with a twinkle!" When she found his picture for me in an old book I could see both—the Moses and the twinkle. "He was one who kept things in balance," she said, "with a blend to his sermons that was—"

The phone rang. By the time she had finished talking her mind had gone on to another subject and I never did hear more of her grandfather. It didn't matter, for I felt sure that the best of him had been built into her.

We talked about death as people contemplating a visit to a distant land might talk.

"It's bound to be the greatest of all journeys," she said. "At seventy-five I find myself looking at life with wondrous intensity, the way a child looks at the little and the big, for there's no difference. What has been happening to make value so definite, so intrinsic, I ask myself. And the answer I come up with is living, the living of life. When you think that it takes nine months to grow a baby, it's not surprising that it takes seventy years and more to grow a soul."

She told me of her husband's death. "All those good years of marriage with their glory and tenderness, and suddenly there was no future. He was at home and I was sitting beside his bed. The end must have come about two in the morning and I knew that the next step was to call the doctor and the undertaker, but why bother them at such a time, I thought. Morning will come soon enough. So I sat beside Chris, everything in me rebelling at what had happened.

"Light began to filter through the room, dispelling night. I went to the door to open it to the spring morning and saw a marvel—our little scraggly pear tree had burst into bloom! Truly it seemed an omen. Chris had spoken often of the pears his father had raised, and prized and tenderly cared for back home in Denmark. This poor little neglected tree was far different from those in Kolding. In fact, we had barely noted that it was a pear when we moved in the autumn before. Undoubtedly the developing buds had been there through the warm days of early spring, but I had not used that side door nor noticed the tree, so as I came on it then it seemed like a sign of God's reassuring love. I knew then I could travel the road however long it might be, for somehow I would never be really alone. Everything would be all right, and just possibly I might still be useful."

"Do you dream of Chris?"

"Once, and I felt his kiss on my lips. It was real and it was enough." She looked at me searchingly and I knew there was something she wanted to share with me. "It's a curious thing," she went on, "but all during the years of my ministry I have known, before ever being informed by a telegram or a telephone call or a neighbor knocking on the door, that a loved friend or one of my people here has died. One particular time there were waves of wonderful fragrance.

"That was truly strange," she said thoughtfully, "for I had not known of this man's illness. He was a sweet person, very much handicapped, living out his life mostly in a wheelchair, attended by his worn and patient little wife who had to have strength for them both though she looked as if any passing breeze would carry her off. The call came from the undertaker, as I remember it, about ten in the morning, asking me if I could take the service as planned, two days later. He had added to his request, 'The widow told me how much you had always meant to Horace.' This was news to me. I had tried to call

"NOT FOR SISSIES" 29

with some regularity in the little home but I hadn't realized at all that I had meant anything special to him, but when I telephoned his wife a little later in the day she said, 'Don't you remember the small Madonna picture you gave him for Christmas?' Well, yes, I did remember, but it must have been all of twenty years ago. His wife had placed it on the mantel shelf in the kitchen where he sat all day in his chair so he could look at it.

"Then I realized with a shock that it was that morning as I ate breakfast that an amazing fragrance of flowers had seemed to be coming into the room in waves. A friend with me at the time hadn't smelled it, but to me it was quite overpowering and unlike anything I had ever experienced before. I did remember, though, that a cousin had told me of the same sort of fragrance coming to her when her parents died. And so, just in case, I checked the time with the hospital. They were perfectly willing to tell me the time of Horace's death and it coincided exactly with the flooding perfume in my kitchen that morning. Well, that happened only once, but the sense of unearthly clarity is so sure that I've come to depend on it."

"Are you excited about your own death?"

She weighed my words before she answered them.

"No, not excited. But content. Whether it

comes easily or with pain, in sleep or with violence like an accident, it will be right. I think we will know when the moment draws near and it will be all that matters. We'll drop everything and go."

"I'd like a bit of warning," I said, "so I could tidy things up, leave my desk in order, you know."

Her laugh was robust. "That might be stalling."

I had to agree.

The hands of the little clock were drawing near to three. I knew she had another appointment and I had a long way to go down the coast. We smiled at each other, indicative of a continuation another time.

Standing by the door as I was getting ready to go out in the rain she exclaimed, "Isn't it wonderful the way God takes care of everything, all the little details, from galaxies to your getting here today!"

Head Into the Wind

ALLEN W. CLARK

*F*og and mist rolled away during the night. My drive down the coast and into New Hampshire was made in bright sunshine. I hoped I might be fortunate enough to find the Clarks at home, as my route lay almost by their door. Stopping to phone along the way, I received a typical response from Allen: "Of course. We're always home except when we're away. Come for lunch, it will be ready when you get here."

The Clarks and Margaret Henrichsen had long been friends. Their denominations differed, and while Margaret had gone into the ministry in her middle years after the death of her husband, Allen had been practically born to the ministry and all his working life Doris had been beside him. Stalwart companion and energetic needler as she had always been, she was in her own right an artist in oils and water color.

In less than an hour I was there. As I drove up to the small old house Allen was just coming from the vegetable garden with a head of late lettuce in his hands. "How about putting a couple of winter squashes in your car?" he asked.

It goes against my nature to refuse anything offered me, but I had to tell him that we had just harvested thirty-two from our own garden. "Allen, you look great!"

"You look as if God had been good to you, too," he said as we shook hands.

Tall, slender, silver-haired, with ruddy cheeks and lively eyes, he was as hearty and hale as I remembered him to be. Little different, in fact, from other times I had seen him across the years. The same, but better, for life's burnishing process always improves when the material to be worked on is sound. Doris came out then, smiling and sprightly. Her brown hair now fairly well streaked with gray, her brown eyes warm as ever, her comfortable figure enveloped in an apron.

"This is good," she said. "This day, and now you!"

When we went in, the house looked as I had remembered it: overflowing with love and evidences of communication with the events of the world and the life of the mind. There were books, papers, piles of letters, paintings, pictures of family and friends, plants. I wondered if there could possibly be room for one more thing, but well I knew that Allen and Doris could always make room for the new book, the old friend.

Realizing that my time was limited, we went

out to the porch on the shady side of the house and sat down at a table that had an abundance of good things already on it. An inquisitive chipmunk, working outside to fill his hole with seeds from a bird-feeder, stopped every now and then to peer up at us. I'm sure he was saying in chipmunk language, "Nothing you have could possibly compare with what I'm storing up against the winter."

Allen started to serve a chicken casserole that looked and smelled delectable. "You're hungry?"

"I am! Breakfast was a long time ago in Damariscotta and the drive has been beautiful. Just seeing so much and getting out now and then to explore has made me ravenous."

"And you like to eat." Allen said it as a compliment.

"I do. Didn't you know that when Bill once analyzed my handwriting he found it revealed that?"

The Clarks laughed. "But you've kept your figure."

"Thanks." My mind hurtled back to my days of Greek and to the teacher who gave us something about the way of life as well as the language. Down the years I have heard her voice stressing the great Greek virtue, moderation—in everything, not just the obvious one of food. "I try," I said.

But it was going to be hard at this meal. There

was a huge bowl of salad, all from the garden with the morning's dew beneath the dressing, then a blueberry pie, and coffee in a pot that never knew what it was to be empty. And to think, I might have been eating a hamburger at McDonald's! How had Doris done it? I'd given them only an hour's notice.

"Do you live like this all the time?"

They looked at each other surprised, as if to say, "If life has good things, why limit the Giver?"

Our conversation flowed fast and I felt as if involved in the assembling of one of their annual letters to their many friends, letters that begin with the salutation

** Happy Easter ** Merry Christmas ** Joyful Thanksgiving **

They talked about the family, the married children and their children; they talked about their work: Doris and her interests, many of them centered in the small town of Sanbornville, the library, the church, the historical society, and especially her paintings; Allen with his work on *Home Prayers*, the weekly ministry-by-mail to churches and housebound folk that he has been carrying on for fifty years. Retired from the actual ministry some time ago, he is often called on to preach at different churches or to take over a parish while the rector is on vacation.

"A high point for me this summer," Allen said, "was in July when I preached at St. Thomas's in Hanover for the first time in forty-four years. St. Thomas's and Beaver Meadow, a tiny chapel across the Connecticut River in the hills of Norwich, Vermont, constituted my first parish, and it was at Beaver Meadow that *Home Prayers* actually began."

"Tell me about it."

So Allen, in his fluent way, told me of the Sunday afternoon services in the little chapel. Attendance was sparse in the winter months, for the flock was scattered and snowdrifts often kept people home. "I was concerned that I was not providing the worship that I should, but on my calls during the second summer I found an answer to my problem."

In every household, usually on the kitchen table, the young minister saw a Sears, Roebuck or a Montgomery Ward catalog. If people could shop by mail, could they not worship by mail? The following winter he planned one service a month in the chapel and on the other Sundays mailed to people a simple service for home worship. A return postcard was included, and people were asked to tell how many had attended worship in that house, and to add some news of the family. Soon there was an excellent "congregation by mail," some twenty-five to forty people all worshipping in their homes.

"From that small start," Allen concluded, "*Home Prayers* branched out to all sorts of people not free to get to church—shut-ins, Sunday workers, young people away in school or college or in the armed services. Today, some twenty-three thousand go out weekly to nine hundred churches. *Home Prayers* has never sent a bill and has always been able to pay its bills from the contributions received."

"My high point," Doris carried on as she slid another piece of blueberry pie onto my plate, "was a few weeks ago when we were in Maine. While walking along the beach, I found some Irish moss that had been washed up by a storm. I gathered as much as we could carry and brought it home to dry. It makes delicious blanc mange. Stay over and I'll give you some tonight for supper."

"What I found on the beach was an idea for a sermon, and for one of the coming issues of *Home Prayers*."

Doris laughed. "He does that all the time, always has."

"Tell me."

"Perhaps it was because Doris and I had been talking about the state of the world that I was especially sensitive. And the problems are legion, even though one's own inner world may have attained some tranquillity. There are people without jobs, people on slender incomes trying to stand up to nightmare prices; problems to which nobody has the answers. And then I saw the weathervane—"

"There it was," Doris interrupted, "on the spire of a little white church in the village where we were staying."

"It gave me an answer," Allen went on. "No matter how hard the wind blows, and it was blowing a gale that day, the weathervane faces into it. It doesn't turn its back to the storm, it faces the storm." He paused.

"Now you'll get the sermon," Doris said aside to me. Her lips might smile but there was pride in her eyes.

"Our cue is to learn from the weathervane. When the storm is at its height, head into it! A frightening choice may strike you like a seventy-mile-an-hour gale; face it and be safe. If you were out on a lake in a canoe and a squall hit, you'd head your bow into the wind and keep afloat. It's the same when a squall of conflicting desires, will against will, strikes a household."

I nodded. I have had little experience on the ocean, but plenty with a canoe on inland waters.

Allen, the minister, went on to his analogy. "The life of Jesus shows us what happened when the winds turned. There had been a wonderful time of teaching, healing, being followed by multitudes; then storm clouds gathered and even his close friends deserted him. He knew that he had to go to Jerusalem and face his enemies. And he did. In time his followers learned to head into the wind. When they did, they kept right side up and rode through the turbulence like the strong vessels that they were."

"Don't forget the lobster boats," Doris reminded.

"Oh, yes. That night in Maine, looking out across the small harbor, I saw that the lobstermen had tied their motorboats to their moorings with strong manila ropes. Each boat swung easily and surely on the water, still facing into the wind though it had diminished greatly at sunset. That was the real lesson for me, and I use it every night almost like an exercise. When sleep doesn't come readily, I tie up my life to the love of God and I know my safety."

"And he goes to sleep," Doris added.

"And when you wake up in the morning?" I asked.

"I'm right side up and ready for another day's living."

I made a mental note to remember this the next time someone said to me, "I can't ever seem to get a night's good sleep any more."

"Perplexing and vexing as the days may be, it's a great time to be alive," Allen said.

I told them of a friend I had visited recently on her eightieth birthday. She had small use for congratulations on an achievement of living.

" 'What I'm doing with this new year,' she said to me, 'is dedicating it to the art of being.' "

"She's got her sights set right," Doris agreed.

"And what's more," I went on, "she told her doctor that he had to keep her going until she was ninety because she was so interested to see what was going to happen to the world in the next ten years."

"It won't be just up to her doctor."

"She knows that, really. But what is ahead for us? for the world?" I looked at Doris, then at Allen.

"I can answer more easily for myself than for the world," he said. "I know that I want to live more intensely every day—see the beauty, feel the suffering, hear the laughter as well as the tears, and try to do something where I am and where I can. Whether I'm growing squash or preparing a sermon, I want to put more of my whole self into it. If I'm anchored, like those lobster boats, and not afraid, I'll be able to trust God for this world and the world to come."

I turned to Doris. "If you knew you had only a little time left, what would you do with it?"

There was gentleness in her eyes but determination in her words: "Mend my relationships."

We had begun the meal with a blessing of Allen's; we were ending it with a grace of silence. Perhaps that was why we soon found ourselves talking about meditation.

"One of the really heartening things today is the growing interest in meditation," Doris began, "particularly among young people. And it's resulting in an increase in mental alertness and a decrease in physical tension. At least, so a doctor friend tells me."

"You mean it makes people more relaxed and able to cope with pressures?" I asked.

"That's a visible sign," Allen said. "An invisible one is that people are getting better at doing one thing at a time, instead of trying to do half a dozen. That's something the years put upon us willy-nilly because we have only enough energy for one thing at a time, but it's a lesson worth learning."

When I asked about Rick, their younger son and the only member of the family's second generation whom I knew, Allen told me a charming story.

"At the time that Rick and his wife were expecting their third child, I asked him how much he cared whether it was a boy or a girl. 'Not much, really,' Rick replied, 'only if it is a boy, I'd be glad because he and I might have as much fun together as we've had, Dad.' It was a boy. Eleven years later I went out on the golf links one summer morning with Rick and his son, Ted. It was the same links on which Rick and I had had many a battle, with zest and militant ribbing, only this time I rode in a caddy cart. There was plenty of banter, with Rick in the parental role. It was a memorable morning. I saw a dream coming true. They were having as much fun as Rick and I had had a couple of decades ago. Oh, there are great and golden moments as one grows older, plenty of them."

"Being with you both sends me back to Browning and his assurance that the best is yet to be."

Stories come easily to Allen, and soon he was off on another. "A few years ago Dick Ellery, a gifted and deeply sensitive painter, did my portrait. I felt that he was not really seeing me because at the time my life was dragging and I was living under clouded skies. As I saw the portrait take shape on the canvas, I exclaimed, 'Dick, you aren't painting the face you see before you. You're painting the best self of a man you've known for thirty years!' And he smiled and said, 'That's exactly what I'm doing.' When he left the portrait in our living room, I took a long look at it and said to myself, 'If a man like that sees gifts in me as he has, why not accept his vision with joy and stop being heavy-hearted?' I'm glad you remembered Browning because when he said 'the best is yet to be' he probably had in mind the best that had been and was being."

"You're putting my random thoughts into words, Allen," I said, "because I have a strong feeling that there won't be any best unless we live up to our best every day."

It was time for me to go. If Doris had let me help with the dishes I might have stayed a little longer, but she wouldn't.

"You've no idea how much fun we have when we do them," she said. "We go over everything talked about and think of more things to talk about."

So we went outdoors together, past late flowers still blooming, and stood for a moment in the warm sun and brisk wind.

Allen raised a weather finger. "It's coming from the southwest. You'll be facing right into it all the way home."

There was fragrance on the air, that subtle compound of autumn—grapes ripening along stone walls, leaves drying, apples reddening. Doris was the first to sense it and she breathed deeply as if to make it part of her.

Allen said, "May your drive home be spiced with heavenly surprises."

So I got into the car and left, but before I was out of sight I looked back. They were standing there smiling, with the wind tossing about them and their hands waving.

"God bless!" they called.

When I turned on to the road, they would turn back to their kitchen. How long had they been doing dishes together? Actual time was of little account. They lived in a blessed Now.

Five Apples a Day

DAN BARRY

*I*t was a glory of an early fall day when I went over the mountain to the near township of Temple for some apples, but even more for a talk with Dan Barry than for apples.

"Come on up to the orchard," he said, "and see for yourself what the crop is this year."

The orchards are all around him so we needn't have stirred more than a few feet from his century-old house and barn, but when we got up to the high open field I knew why he wanted to go there. The view took in hundreds of apple trees and a rim of mountains, not high by some standards but high enough to give the feel of a protective embrace. On the distant hills, maples had turned red and gold, beeches were showing copper tinges, oaks had yet to change. The bright colors were set off by the green of pines and hemlocks and the intense blue of the sky. The whitest of clouds raced and changed shapes as if the breeze was playing a game with them.

That was the far view. The near one was of

trees heavy with ripening apples, red or yellow, and some mixed. It wasn't just a sight for the eyes: fragrance was on the air. There were large boxes set at intervals, and ladders against some of the trees. Pickers working stopped long enough to wave to Dan, and he responded. I filled my eyes with the distant paisleyed beauty of the hills. I breathed the pungent air. I bit into an apple that I had been feeling for its roundness. I listened as Dan talked. In one small moment of time, on one small piece of green turf, all my senses were involved.

Dan talked about the trees as if each one was a member of his family.

"How many?" I asked.

"Oh, twenty-four hundred, more or less, but I don't count them; if I do I lose one or two. And some go every year, but we set out new ones to keep ahead. Mice are the real problem. See, there's a tree they got last winter, girdling it under the snow. And look over there, that's where we set out three new trees. They're Macouns and will bear in another two years. Now, if they'd been Baldwins we'd have to wait twenty years for a crop and it would be just half of what McIntosh and Macoun bring, bushel for bushel.

"Deer are a problem, too. They come out of the woods and do they like apples! Not just the drops they paw for over the ground. I've seen them lift their heads and pick apples right off the branches, just the way that fellow on the ladder is doing over there." Dan chuckled and pushed his battered felt hat back on his head. The way he spoke made me feel that he was willing to share.

"But it's the weather that really runs your business. When it's with you, you've got a good year. This is a good year. Every one of those trees you're looking at will be yielding forty bushels or better."

Dan was born in Temple in the early 1890's. He never had any doubt but that it was the best town in the United States, so there was no reason to leave it. He went to school in nearby Wilton because the one-room schoolhouse not far from his home closed when the school board refused to raise the teacher's salary to three dollars a week. By fourteen he was farming, helping his father and getting ready to take the place over sometime. Chickens were the mainstay, then a milking herd of Holsteins, and gradually apples.

"When I was a boy and picked blueberries," Dan explained, "I vowed then that I'd go in to something bigger, and I did. Had about a hundred trees in 1920 and each one gave me fifty bushels. With more trees we don't get quite so many apples, tree for tree, but they're doing all right. I lease the orchard now, except for about three hundred trees that I keep for myself." He pushed his hat further back on his head and gave the smile a Yankee will when he knows he's got himself a good trade. "When the men come in to prune and fertilize and spray the trees, they do mine too. And, early in the season when the hives are brought in, the bees don't know my trees from theirs. They work hard, those bees, for the bloom of the different varieties keeps coming along just a few days apart."

Hard worker himself, his admiration for the bees was in his tone.

"That's a cute color," he pointed to a tree with the reddest of red apples. "Some of those will be five-inchers and weigh a pound apiece." Then he pointed to a tree of Golden Delicious. "I used to think they were the best of all, but we've got a cross called Red-gold. Never tasted anything better."

I wanted to know what made them so good. Was it the soil? the clear air? the surround of hills? My questions tumbled out and I wasn't sure whether he really heard me or whether I should expect answers. Behind his glasses his gray eyes, faded by time, didn't seem to see me. But he saw and he had heard.

"There's water in this land, a river of water far down under your feet. I know because I've been over every foot of it with a dowser. When I saw the willow stick bend in his hand time and time again I wanted to try it. At first it didn't work for me, but I guess he charged my batteries because it works now. There's water enough to draw the roots down and give the trees deep drinking when the rains are short. And, another thing, this land is high. We don't get the early frosts that the farms in the valley do."

I thought of what he had said about weather running your business and realized that he had a built-in insurance against summer drought and early freeze.

"And the air is different, there's no doubt about that." He told me of a man, a Civil War veteran, who had worked in a factory in Wilton and gone short on sleep because of the close air of the town. "I said to him, 'You drive up here after work and take yourself to the edge of the field where it meets the orchard and wrap yourself up in a blanket. You'll sleep all right when night comes down and I'll come along in the morning to tickle your toes so you can get down to work on time.' He did just that and got good sleep whenever he needed it. Added years to his life.

"Men from the State university come here to show me some new things about apple culture, and there are some old things that I can show them. You know, there're tricks to everything and you learn as you go along. But you have to do some thinking to keep up with the new ways, and just because they're new doesn't always mean they're better. I'm for light pruning in the early spring and in the fall I leave apples on the trees for color, and fertilize well all season to sweeten the taste. Heavy doses of potash are good for color, too, and nitrogen for growth; but there's nothing like cow manure when you have it handy or can get it. It's like dessert for the trees. You know yourself, if you have a fellow working for you you've got to feed him good. Trees are just the same. Look over there, ever see anything prettier than those yellow plum trees? And the fruit tastes like honey.

"A man came to see me one day and said he couldn't understand why he had just little apples on his trees. I told him what I did and he said, 'That must cost you fifty cents a day for every tree. I couldn't afford that.'" Dan chuckled. " 'That's no economy,' I told him. 'You've got to give the best to get the best.' "

His gaze ranged. I felt it resting proudly, even tenderly, on all the trees he could see and the hundreds that were out of sight. "If you're going to make an orchard pay," he said, and he was serious, "you've got to sweat."

Dan put it in a word. I knew from what a friend had told me that Dan was up with the sun and to bed at dusk during the season, and from first pruning to last harvesting that would be a good three-fourths of the year. He looked as if it hadn't hurt him any and as if he'd had a lot of fun.

"You know, it's true, that old saying about an

apple a day, only I'll settle for five or six. There's no better medicine. People get their veins and arteries all plugged up from rich living. Why, I had a man here whose doctor sent him up for the air, said he couldn't work because he had a bad heart. It wasn't long before he was eating apples instead of ice cream, then picking a hundred bushels a day right alongside of me. By the time he went back to the city, his heart was as sound as mine. His doctor said so, wrote me a letter as a testimonial. I read an article in the paper the other day about the states where there is the most heart trouble, and they're where apples are scarce. Now, you take that Vitamin E that's found in apples, and emulsify it—"

But I never did get the end of that story, for something caught his eyes and he wanted to be sure that I would see it, too. "There now, over there, did you ever see anything prettier in all your life?"

It was a tree heavy with apples, their red glowing in the late long rays of the sun.

"They'll be ready for picking in another couple of weeks. Come back then and have yourself a box."

We started down the grassy path toward the house where maple trees returned the sun's color like a compliment.

Talking all the time, Dan suddenly exclaimed and drew my attention to the sight he must have seen countless times in the years he had lived there, married, brought up his family, carried on when alone. But the words he used were Whittier's words describing autumn's varied glory.

And then he moved into some favorite lines from Gray's "Elegy": " 'The curfew tolls the knell of parting day,/Now all the air a solemn stillness holds.' " He skipped over and through some of the verses but his memory, far sharper than mine, served him well and the imagery matched the scene. " '. . . the genial current of the soul . . . scatter plenty o'er the land.' " He sighed happily. "I like to have words like that in my mind when I'm working around the trees. Now, next year—" and he started to tell me some of his plans for another harvest.

After I left, a line from the "Elegy" came into my mind, "How jocund did they drive their team afield!" That word *jocund* seemed to belong to Dan Barry, for there was as much of cheer in its sound as in its meaning. When I got home and could refresh my memory with the dictionary, I discovered that the Latin root of jocund means *to help*. No need to ask Dan what's ahead for him: the best apples that can be grown and better health for everyone.

A few weeks later his daughter, Mary, brought me a huge bag of five-inch Macouns mixed with her father's current favorite Red-golds. In her much younger face I saw the strong lines of her father's, in the rich tones of her voice I heard him all over again. "Oh, he loves life, he does indeed!"

"And he isn't afraid to work hard."

Mary chuckled. "Not he." The sound was so like her father's voice he might have been in the room with us.

"J Make a Little Joke"

ANNA YOSS

*A*nna Yoss and I talk often together, but I call her "Grandmother" as do generations of people who know her, not only her grandchildren and great-grandchildren but the people who have come to her restaurant over the years.

The one she now has, Grandmother's House, is off a winding road out of the village of Francestown and under the shadow of Crotched Mountain. A small brown farmhouse, it is framed by the greenest of lawns. There are flowers blooming in trim beds and hanging baskets—geraniums, petunias, and those that will give color over a long season. A pond is near. Six white geese and one small multi-colored duck glide through its water, then waddle up to the house, front door or back, for their occasional feed of bread or corn. There is a field in which two fat ponies graze. At the door a handsome German shepherd greets visitors with dignity.

Inside there is warmth and cheer in the winter, cool comfort in the summer, and always flowers, candlelight, sparkling silver and shining glass. The dining room is not large, and there is a smaller one in the rear. Almost everyone comes by reservation and is a frequent guest. At some time during the diners' visits, Grandmother comes from the kitchen in a fresh-looking cotton dress. She stops at table after table, sometimes sitting down if time allows to join in a cup of coffee. Always her first question is the same, "It was good? You would like some more?"

But this was a day when she came to my house to see me.

We sat by the fire, sipped coffee and ate ginger sandwiches which she pronounced good. Talking together, she took me back to the turn of the century and the small town near Weimar in East Germany where her father had a large productive farm. Some forty workers were employed on it and there were cows, sheep and pigs, chickens and geese, fields, pastures and many buildings. For Annchen and her brother Werner the years of their growing up on the farm were good years. Grandmother paused, reaching for a word, then said, "Gemütlich." It is a word for which English has no equivalent.

It was not only in school that her education came. Much of it was gained at home in house and kitchen, dairy and garden. " 'You may never have to do any of this,' my mother used to say, 'but by learning how you will be able to show others.' Ja, ja," Grandmother smiled and accented her words firmly, "I can hear my mother saying to me, 'Whatever is done, do it right.' "

Christmas was the happiest time of the year. Anna and Werner were home from school, cousins were there, aunts and uncles; everyone was together. They would go to church in the carriage drawn by two spanking black horses, with the coachman sitting atop on the box. When they came home her father would take the children for a long walk, through the fields and the barns. Returning to the house, there was the tree glowing with lights, and presents on the table.

"The Lutheran church we went to was the one where Bach once played the organ. I liked the pastor. His sermons gave me something to think about all day. Once, when I was a little girl, I asked him what people meant when they talked about faith. He said, 'If you stood in play on your dining room table and your father said *Anna, jump!* you would jump, knowing his arms were there to catch you. You would believe without asking. So it is in life, but it is God's arms that are there to catch us, even more—to embrace us.' Never did I forget those words.

"Now I will say for you my favorite line from *William Tell*." She gave it first in German, then repeated it in English, " 'What we inherit from our parents, we have to work to make our own.' "

"You did."

"Ja!" She went back over the events that finally brought her to this country—the deaths of her parents, the sale of the farm, her marriage to Paul Yoss and the births of their three daughters. In the 1920's there was little future in Germany and, though times were difficult in the United States, there was more hope. Werner left first to establish himself in hotel work in New Jersey, Paul followed, and after some time she arrived with the children. They became American citizens and soon had their own restaurant in the country. There she was able to prove something long felt: "for good food people will go anywhere." The work was hard, the hours were long, but in cooking, serving and getting to know people, Anna Yoss found what she most liked to do. She ended her account of the years with her familiar "Nicht?"

"Grandmother, do you think in German?"

"No, no, in English. But I do my accounts in German." She smiled, a curious little smile that seemed to indicate she was letting me into her confidence. "I pray in German."

We fell silent for a moment. I got up to put another log on the fire and refill her coffee cup.

The next story in the chapter I knew, for it was when my life and hers overlapped. She came to southern New Hampshire to own and operate a large inn. Soon it was widely known that there was no food like hers in all the countryside, no service to equal hers. Interested in everyone who came to her, she made her customers her friends and in time they made her life. She needed them. With the passing of the years Paul had died, then Werner, and the daughters were married, with homes and families of their own.

When she was seventy she took a step that many take at that age—she retired—but she soon reversed it. People were her life; without them, and doing for them, there was nothing. The inn had been sold, but there was a little one in the shadow of a mountain up for sale. She bought it, and "fixed it up so everything would be just so," and called it Grandmother's House. More often than not there were grandchildren with her to help and to enjoy the country life. She delighted in them and said they kept her young. Long-time friends soon found her out in the new location; she knew their ways, and they liked that. Others often had to learn her ways and discover what was expected of them.

"Sometimes I have to say to them, 'In this room you wear a coat and tie, you can do as you like in the other room.' They do not mind. I make a little joke of it and say that I am, perhaps, old-fashioned, nicht? But here in my house a rule is a rule."

One of her rules is that only the best will ever be used, the best meat, the best fruits, and all in season as much as possible. It is the only way she knows to get the best results. "I am not in business to get rich, but to please people."

She told me of something that had happened the previous Saturday. "They came, five of them, and they are among my favorite people. They said it was to celebrate their daughter's sixteenth birthday and they were counting on my chocolate cake, but—they had forgotten to make a reservation and I did not expect them. I did not know!"

This, I knew, was drama of the highest order, but I also knew that because Grandmother was the chief actor all would somehow be well. She laughed, allaying the suspense she had me in.

"So, I went back to the kitchen and made the cake between the first course and the dessert, and they were happy."

I felt like having "a little joke" with her. "Grandmother, if someone left you a million dollars, what would you do?"

"Find some good use for it. I would not sit around."

"And you'd keep on working?"

"Ja, ja. You learn more from life if you work."

Her days are long: planning, buying, preparing, cooking, with a sharp eye always out for the work done by those in her employ. When it is over and she is alone, the tables set for the next day, the pots and pans ready for more cooking, she sits down at her desk and does her accounts.

"It may be midnight then, and my legs ache from standing so long, but sleep does not come easily to me so why should I not work?" She leaned toward me. "Do you think there will be sweat in Heaven?"

Had I not had an affirmative answer to both questions, I felt that I would go down in her estimation. With many of us who know her, it means a good deal to stand high with her. Then I asked her if she ever took time for herself.

"Oh, ja," she said emphatically, and her eyes opened wide. "I have Monday to myself. That is the day when the House is closed."

"What do you do?"

"I come and have coffee with you, and those little ginger sandwiches which are now all gone."

"But on other Mondays?"

"I enjoy my home. I water my flowers and clean my house. I do my bookkeeping and brush my dog. I read a book."

"And your special joy, what is it?"

A smile spread slowly over her face. "My family and my customers," she said simply, "making people happy."

Awake the Dawn

EVE DAWSON

*O*ctober's extravaganza of color and windswept untidiness had given way to the austere neatness of November. Leaving New Hampshire behind me and heading into Vermont, the hills were slate blue against a clear sky. Fields were brown with drying grass. On the edge of a woodland or up a slope the nearly burned-out candles of larches gave a dim glow. Everything in nature said that winter was near; but suddenly it was spring again when Eve Dawson opened her door in answer to my knock.

Within a moment I felt embraced by light and beauty, and that sudden excitement that happens rarely in life: here was someone whom I had never met before and yet it was as if I had always known her. Even as we shook hands I felt that with her I could be completely myself. In a few days she would be leaving Vermont for the winter in New York. I wanted to talk with her and had asked for an hour of her time. The clock was striking eleven as I entered.

Slender, with cornflower-blue eyes, a rose-tinged skin, fair hair and a lovely smile, she took my hand and drew me into the room. She wore a cotton dress of a flowery print and an old red corduroy jacket. She asked me where my dog was and, if possible, I felt even more at home when we discovered that we shared a like feeling for Shelties.

"We had our Bramble for sixteen years," she said. "I'll show you her picture, such a sensitive and loving friend. One morning she came up to our room and looked at me in a special way, then she dropped to the floor, crossed her paws, and life was over. That was beautiful."

The blue eyes had misted but the smile remained. I felt that everything in Eve Dawson's life was caressed by beauty, even the death of a dearly loved dog.

"Will you have some tea?"

"Yes, indeed, I'd love to have some."

So I sat down by a table with books spread out on it and let my eyes roam around the room while she disappeared behind some curtains where a kettle could be heard coming up to the boil.

The room was large enough for living and for exhibitions in the summer; there was another room adjacent for a gallery, and a stairs leading up. On the walls were her paintings, some impressionistic, some realistic: flowers, landscapes in all seasons, city scenes, people. Each one had a quality of light, an exuberance of joy. I could well understand why the Grist Mill Gallery in Chester Depot was affectionately called "the garden of Eve."

I knew she had been an accomplished actress in England, that she had come to the United States in the 1930's, that she had married a distinguished architect. I knew, too, that her painting was a career embarked on only some twenty years ago, but that she had become one of the most sought-after and most bought of the artists in the Southern Vermont School. Many awards had come to her, and she had had several shows in New York City as well as Vermont. She and her husband had bought the old grist mill and made it into a gallery to show and sell work of artists of the region, and stimulate more work. And I knew that James Dawson had died in 1970. The structure of a life, I thought to myself; but it's what's between the lines that make it life.

It was good to have had those moments of retrospect while she was getting the tea, because as soon as she came and sat down on the low couch beside me and started talking, we never stopped. Looking at her, I saw someone vibrant and sure. I felt her strength, but it was her gentleness that charmed me.

"I'm glad we've met, but why did you want to see me?" she asked.

I told her about my conversations. Her eyes widened. A child would say with shining eyes, "Today I am ten years old," for the marvel of adding another digit was the fact. She said, with her blue eyes shining, "I'm in my eightieth year." There was delight in the way she said it.

Her childhood in England, in the county of Somerset, was a sheltered one. A delicate state of health and a timid nature kept her home with a nurse and governess. By the time the Great War was over, the social upheaval that England went through changed for many the whole pattern of life. Eve was nearing twenty and aware that she would have to do something with her life. There was little that her education had equipped her to do, but she had a trained mind, a good voice, an adaptable nature. The stage was one place where such accomplishments might be put to use. Dreading the exposure, she felt that acting would compel her to overcome her innate timidity.

I thought to myself: so exquisite now, what must the beginning have been? And I saw her as a Gloriana among girls.

Her first years were spent as an understudy. The stage became for her a proving ground. It gave her a great deal of travel outside England, it also provided the opportunity to meet people. Drawn into many different kinds of situations, she learned how to rise to occasions as they came along.

"Oh, but there was one that I was completely unprepared for!" she exclaimed, with a little laugh that had in it as much of intimacy as it did of innocence. "It was at a party one night in London, after a show. A man, a very nice man and quite handsome, slipped a note into my hand. When I had a chance to read it, it said 'I love you.' I couldn't understand what it meant and later asked him about it. 'Just what it says. I want to marry you.'"

The man was James Dawson, a young Scottish architect who had already done some notable buildings in Great Britain and would soon be doing more in the United States.

Three years went by before they were married. His career took him to New York and her career took her there, too, not as an actress but as an assistant in the Elizabeth Arden Beauty Salon. In 1933 they were married, and for many years they lived on Sutton Place sharing life blissfully.

"Bramble, our merle Sheltie with the handsome white ruff, was a part of those years. There was a host of friends and frequent travel. I'm sure we would have loved children, had they come to us, but we had each other. Jimmie used to sing the old Scottish songs to me. I can hear him now, especially the one of Bobbie Burns' that ends 'I will love thee still, my dear, 'til all the seas gang dry.'"

Contrast to New York, yet complement, too, in

its peaceful stimulus, were the summers spent in Vermont. They found an old farmhouse, enjoyed restoring it, and enjoyed even more sharing it with their friends. It was home for twenty-five years until the grist mill was bought, then that became home and gallery, too.

"And now you're an artist! Tell me how it all happened."

She laughed, a sound like grace notes in the music of her voice. "One day, when Jimmie was doing a rush job for a hospital, I was waiting for him in his office. He gave me his watercolors to pass the time, and though I'd had some lessons in England years ago, I'd never really done anything with watercolor. When Jimmie had finished his work and looked at my doodles he exclaimed, 'If I could put color on like that, I'd make it my whole job!' So, when a friend in Vermont asked me to join a group to paint outdoors under the tutelage of Harry Shokler, I gladly went along. It was Harry Shokler, of Vermont and Grand Central Galleries in New York, who made me promise to go to the Art Students League when I returned to New York."

"And you did?"

"Oh yes, and there followed wonderful years under great teachers—George Grosz, Harry Sternberg, Margery Ryerson. The League was still feeling the impact made by Robert Henri. He had helped students break through timidity

AWAKE THE DAWN 65

and traditionalism, and his book helped me. Do you know it, *The Art Spirit*, edited by Margery Ryerson?"

I nodded. It had long been one of my favorites.

"It was hard work, oh, unbelievably hard work, to put on canvas what my outer eye saw clearly and my inner eye was transmuting. But almost from the start I had the feeling that I was doing good work, not with reason but with passion. My talent, such at it was, had been little suspected; but once discovered, I felt an obligation to perfect it. I've always felt that each person who comes into the world brings some gift. It often takes years to discover it, then hard work and more years to bring it out. But once it is found, the talent must be used or it will rust."

"You were, perhaps, fifty when you discovered your talent?"

"Oh, all of that! But it was Jimmie who started me, that day in his office. Of course, he was biased when he praised my use of color then, but he always was the least critical of men, except of himself. He saw only the good in people and to be quite truthful—" She hesitated.

"Please be truthful," I urged.

"He was the noblest man I ever met. Everyone who knew him loved him. I wish you could have known him."

My eyes went again to the paintings hanging on the white walls of the room in which we sat.

Each one was luminous, as if she was intent on clarifying for other eyes something she had seen and responded to—a snowy road, a pool, quiet pond-lilies, gay daisies, red poppies, people. Light was there, sometimes gentle in its embrace, sometimes bold in its revealing, and each one was held within the design she had conceived for it.

She left me for a moment and returned with two reviews which she put in my hand. One was of an exhibition of several artists at the Southern Vermont Art Center eleven years ago. I read it eagerly: ". . . She cares about light—its tremulous shimmer and stabbing glint. She cares about paint—about shaping crisp or unfurled or delicately convoluted petal forms and textures from vivid pigments with a palette knife. Most of all she cares about the moment, about catching a succession of instants: fixing forever, with chromatic legerdemain, that fraction of a second when light, color, texture, tone and design are in perfect blinding conjunction."

Then I read the second. Both reviews proved for me something I had long felt: that as the years go on, one only becomes more so. In her case, more in command of her craft, more radiant.

"I thought you'd like to see what can be done later in life," she said when I gave the reviews back to her.

In answer, I murmured some favorite words

from Tennyson's Ulysses, " '. . . and tho' we are not now that strength which in old days/Moved earth and heaven . . .' " She joined in with me and we made a little chorus, " 'That which we are, we are; One equal temper of heroic hearts/To strive, to seek, to find, and not to yield.' "

"My Quaker governess taught that to me when I was a little girl," she said. "I'm glad you know it, too."

Dimly I recalled a passage in *The Art Spirit* in which Henri might have been describing Eve Dawson: "I believe that keeping one's faculties in full exercise is the secret of good health and longevity. It made Titian a young man at nearly a hundred. Perhaps mental inactivity is the most fatiguing thing in the world."

Then I told her of a line I had read that morning in the 108th Psalm, the Revised Standard Version throwing a new and lovely light on the older King James translation, "My heart is ready, I will awake the dawn!"

"That's it," she replied, "I'm sure that's it. We move toward the light yet we're in the light. Yes, yes—awake the dawn!"

Looking at her, looking at the paintings on the walls behind her, one then another an adventure, a surprise, I felt that she was one who with each new day made an offering of herself to life—her eyes that they might see beauty, her heart that it might respond, and her hands that they might interpret it in the art form she had made hers.

Eight years had gone by since the Dawsons bought the old grist mill and turned it into a gallery and a home; and six years had passed since Jimmie had died. I asked her if she was ever lonely.

She looked at me as if the word was not in her vocabulary. "With my friends in England? With my friends here? I feel surrounded. But I know what you mean. I keep on keeping on." She talked more about her husband, then said, "Such wonderful years we had together but, when they were over, I felt that if I grieved he would, and I did not want that. Often I sing to myself the old song he used to sing to me—'I will love thee still, my dear, 'til all the seas gang dry.'"

We went out to stand on the balcony in sunshine and sharp wind. The water that had once turned a millwheel tumbled over the dam and made background music to her words.

"When I was a child I had such a fear of death, and it was only because I heard grownups talking about heaven and hell and that some people went one place and some another. That was incomprehensible to me. I wanted to feel that we were all together, all near, not separated. Gradually I overcame that old fear, and perhaps the greatest moment of revelation came when Jimmie passed on. Love had sustained us all our years and love would not stop. I knew I could not lose him. One moment here, the next—" She caught herself. "There isn't even a *there*, it's a continuing. I've dreamed of him, but the dream is more the feeling of a presence than anything visual. And I know, yes I know, that some day I, too, will take that closer walk with God. Before that time comes I want to get more order into my life, tidy up the little things, the odds and ends, so others won't be burdened."

She looked at me. Again her blue eyes held a gentle query, almost as if she wondered if she could trust me.

Everything in me said, "Please."

"This is noteworthy," she began, speaking softly, but her voice carried above the sound of the water. "Before Jimmie passed on, the hymn 'Trust the Eternal' kept coming to my mind over and over, and about a week after his passing a friend took me to church in Woodstock and they sang the same hymn that had been haunting me so persistently, 'Trust the Eternal.' "

She turned and her gaze rested on the flowing water. "The river can run high at times," she said. "There have even been floods across the fields, but this old building is sound as a rock."

And so are you, I thought.

My hour was up. Distantly a clock was striking. We left the balcony, went through the room with the paintings on the walls and I filled my eyes with them again. At the door we did not say goodbye. Our hands clasped, our eyes met, and we said, "Awake the dawn!"

The day might be November as I drove away, but spring was in my heart.

A Cheerful Heart Is a Good Medicine

ERWIN C. MILLER, M.D.

*H*e came into the room with his little dog, Fido, on a crinkly red leash, talking to him all the while. One hand was occupied with the antics of the tiny dog whose pink plastic harness held a lively body in check; the other hand balanced a bright yellow umbrella over one shoulder. And I was a child again. It did not matter what the years said, any more than it mattered that there was no rain to be warded off by the umbrella and no dog at the end of the leash.

Here was a real live clown, dressed in a brilliant multicolored garment like a pajama suit. A huge white ruff went around his neck. On top of his bald head, from which dripped a few strings of red yarn hair, reposed an elegant tall silk hat. A bulbous nose and bright spots of crimson color high on his cheeks completed the illusion. I didn't want to know who he was, because just for then he was all the mirth and magic of childhood, when seeing is believing, when no questions are to be asked, and the ridiculous becomes the real.

Fido, not being there at all except as a figment, was the most wonderful dog in the world: the one, as a child, I had always wanted to have.

The clown took off his top hat with a grand gesture, set the toy umbrella on a chair, and let the leash drop to the floor where it folded itself up near the tiny harness. "Toto," he said, making a slight bow towards me.

How does one address a clown, I wondered. Maestro? Monsieur? Or just by his name?

"Toto," I repeated, acknowledging the bow. "I'm glad to meet you."

"Won't you sit down?"

He waited for me to take my place beside a table which had on it a whole literature of clowning, then he sat opposite me.

So this was Erwin Miller, long-time friend and husband of one of my oldest and dearest friends! I knew he had retired from active medical practice at seventy-seven and that he had resumed a boyhood ambition which had been kept alive through the years, but I had not seen him in action. Secretly I asked myself if he was not making quite as many people well by getting them to laugh as he had long done with diagnoses and prescriptions.

The sun streamed into the room where we sat. Harriet Miller came back from a walk with their handsome collie and gave me some quick items of news about their two married children. Then she said that luncheon would be ready in a little while and she would call us. Still captivated by the apparition before me, I almost did not want to do anything to break the spell. But I did. We started to talk, and went back over the years to Erwin's childhood.

As a small boy growing up in Malone, New York, high in the Adirondack Mountains, he had been fascinated by circuses. Every year the big ones came to Malone, which was at the junction of two major railroads and was the county seat. Erwin could always be sure of going to the circus, since his father was executive director of the fairgrounds. Each circus came for a one-day stand before going on to the next town, but it was a full day. Two shows gave plenty of occasion to laugh and marvel and just plain enjoy. People poured into Malone from all the near villages, and some from many miles away. They arrived by horse and buggy, in farm wagons loaded with children, and in the occasional Model T. And there wasn't one who didn't plan on making a day of it.

Erwin, because of his father, had a chance to meet many of the circus people, not all of the eighteen hundred performers in a typical troupe, but enough to satisfy him, and especially the clowns.

"There was one in particular, his name was Toto. I had tremendous admiration for him and utter delight in watching what he did. Year after year he came. He had an outstanding personality. And what a love for children! He gave his life to making them happy."

"Now you are Toto."

"Yes, I took his name a while ago. Clowns do this, but no one takes another's name while that clown is living. It's one of our unwritten rules."

"How about the animals? Did you get to know them too?"

"Yes, indeed, but not all. There were more than five hundred horses, elephants, tigers, bears, and many other kinds. I liked the well ones, of course, but the sick ones began to mean something to me in a different way."

Caring for sick or hurt creatures was of increasing interest to Erwin, and he talked often with the two veterinarians who traveled with each circus; this led to talking with the two doctors who took care of the people. Differences in treatment, or similarities, prompted him to ask questions. The answers he received only deepened his respect for the complex and wonderful machinery that was the body, whether animal or human.

"It's been the circus for me as long as I can remember. Why," he chuckled, "I had my first date with Harriet when I took her to a circus!"

Christmas and the Fourth of July were the traditional great days in a boy's life, but for Erwin Miller their equals were the days the circus came to town. They began in the morning with the parade through town, and went on to the last moment when the big tent was taken down and the flatcars began to roll away with their freight of people, animals, and properties. From that early hour until long past midnight, everyone worked. Erwin discovered many things that he could do to help, but he never took money for a circus job. After one circus left and while waiting for the sound of another calliope, there were the mountains. During those years of their growing, he and his brother climbed them all.

High school completed, he was accepted at Annapolis and might have had a career in the Navy, but his burgeoning interest in medicine won out. Therefore he went to Dartmouth College, and after receiving his bachelor's degree—which included the first two years of medical school—he remained at the college teaching anatomy and histology for three years. He then transferred to Harvard Medical School, where he received his M.D. degree, and was the Austin Teaching Fellow in Histology and Embryology for two years. This was followed by another two years of training as an intern in internal medicine at the Massachusetts General Hospital in Boston. After completing his internship in 1929 he was persuaded to go to nearby Worcester, there to begin long years of service in his specialty of internal medicine on the staff of the Memorial Hospital.

During the years there were many opportunities for clowning, and he never missed a chance to get to a circus. "I wanted to keep up with the 'joeys' to see what they were doing."

The opportunities to clown increased when he had a small son and daughter and their many friends to entertain. Erwin was a natural; he had never gone to clown school, but close observation and a delight in, and respect for, clowns increased his skills. Never at a loss, he could improvise a clown act at a moment's notice. Harriet recalls the time when they were spending a summer on Cape Cod and there was need for some entertainment. Erwin produced it, acting the part of a ballet dancer complete with tutu—but with a clown's large flat shoes. Making circles with one foot then another, and cutting capers, he had the grownups laughing as gaily as the children.

As an internist whose patients kept in touch with him long after they were well, as a teacher whose medical students caught some of his fire, he liked to acknowledge his debt to clowns. To make people laugh, or try to make them laugh, was a way to help them through dark moments, help them face tough problems. "Every doctor has to have something of the clown in him," he said. "You can't be a sourpuss even when you feel like one."

He was in charge of the festivities, and the formalities, for the fiftieth reunion of his class at Harvard, and did the same job at Dartmouth for his fifty-fifth. After both were accomplished, he began to look forward to retirement and that, for Erwin Miller, meant more clowning than ever. Acting the part was stimulation always; training others to act was equally exciting.

Harriet came in then to sit down with us for a while. Between them they related for me the events of a recent day, sponsored by the Parks Recreation Department, when more than ten thousand children were entertained. The eighteen members of the Clown Club, all of them volunteers moved around in their zany costumes and heavy make-up, doing their pantomimes and pratfalls, telling their jokes, making their magic. The air rang with shouts of glee, shrieks of laughter. One clown after another shook the hands thrust out to them and made sure that no hand went unshaken. "When we got home," Erwin concluded, "I said to Harriet, 'Hasn't this been a wonderful day!'"

But children are not the only ones to be so entertained.

Members of the Clown Club, singly or in groups, and always as volunteers, visit hospitals, homes for the elderly, and go wherever the chance to laugh will do good, relieve tension, and help people to forget themselves for a little while. "The elderly respond as children do," Erwin added, "for a clown appeals to every age, perhaps best to the extremes of age where things can hurt the most and linger long. People need to laugh. It's therapy of a high order."

I told Erwin of an interview with Malcolm Muggeridge that I had seen recently on television. "He said something that made me think of you."

"Was it about clowns?"

"It was, and it came in the middle of a somewhat serious discourse on religion. In answer to a question, Mr. Muggeridge said that he felt the real understanding of God could never be achieved by the intellect. 'It is the mystics, the artists, and the clowns who really know God.' Those were his words and I wrote them down quickly so I could give them to you."

Erwin smiled, not the sad-smile of a clown but the glad-smile of a man whose work is appreciated.

"Where did your costume come from?" I asked.

"Oh, it's mine, all mine, idea and fashioning," he tilted his head toward Harriet to acknowledge her help in it. "A clown's get-up and make-up are what he invents for himself. My little dog, my yellow umbrella, my top hat and red hair are my trademark. No clown would use another's outfit any more than he would use another's gags. He makes his own and keeps adding to them. It's like his name, which is all his and only his."

He talked about clowns he had known, like Emmett Kelly, and others he had seen and admired. Many names were new to me, but to members of any of the nation's clown clubs they would be like patron saints. "There are no age restrictions," he went on. "Anyone who wants to clown is welcome. In our club we have some quite young members, some middling, some—" he paused—"like me. As long as a man is well, can put on his own make-up and invent his gags and costume, he's with us. For the most part, it's ad-libbing, doing what the moment calls for. And with clowns there's never any ridicule, no unkindness. Joey makes people laugh at him, his mournfulness, his awkwardness, his surprised silence. We're always seeking new members, here in Worcester, for there's a need, such a need. So many children haven't had the chance to laugh, so many older people have forgotten how to laugh.

"And there's a real need in circuses. So much so that there's a clown school now in Venice, Florida, near where the Ringlings have their winter quarters. It's a three-month term, ten hours a day, with forty in a class. When they graduate they are real masters, but they have to have the knack to begin with. More than five hundred apply every year, and forty are accepted. Sounds like the Kingdom of Heaven, doesn't it? In the early days clowns were natural-born; now they learn how to make their costumes, to put on their make-up and to do a host of other things like acrobatics and miming."

When we went into the dining room for luncheon, I felt sure that Erwin's nose would interfere with his eating and that he would take it off, but not at all. He was a clown for a day, my day, and nothing would allow him to slip out of character. Our conversation ranged from his days in Labrador with the Grenfell Mission to travels taken with his family; but we kept coming back to clowns.

After luncheon he showed me his bag of tricks. It was a black bag, somewhat smaller than a gladstone, and I wondered if it was the very one he had carried with him when making his house calls, taking from it a doctor's equipment and some simple comforts. Now it overflowed with fun, and as he did his magic for me I laughed and marveled.

I did not want to know how it was that blowing on a colored scarf while twirling it around could make a bunch of paper flowers appear; or how it was that a jar of milk when tipped never spilled; or how a series of separate rings could suddenly be joined into loops like a necklace for an elephant. Sheer buffoonery it was, and I loved it. So much of life is explainable. It was good to laugh at something that one didn't want to have explained.

On my way home through late afternoon sunshine I thought of the children in the park. Words from an interview with Margaret Meade read recently came back to me: "If you want to think about the future you must have children—children in your life," she said. "Your own or borrowed, it doesn't matter, but children. They are the future."

And then absurdly—but not surprisingly, for this had been the tone of the day—I began to sing an old nursery rhyme, paraphrasing it: "Rings on his fingers, bells on his toes," I sang, "he shall have laughter wherever he goes."

Yes, Dr. Miller, and love, too. As evidenced by all those little fluttering hands reaching out to touch the clown who has delighted them.

"And All Shall Be Well"

ELIZABETH GRAY VINING

Over a score of years we have talked together, especially during the long summers she spends in New Hampshire; and we have talked in a variety of places—in a canoe, or while picking blueberries around the same bush, or on the summit of a small mountain when, the climb done, we could throw ourselves down on the turf, settle back against a convenient boulder and gaze across the wide land to distant hills. We have talked in letters. And often in the silences of a long drive something has been said, left for moments, and taken up again to be enlarged on further. What have we talked about? Books, travel, ideas, friends. But more and more, like homing pigeons, our conversations have been coming back to the "last things." We have both lived long enough to be fascinated by what is ahead; not here, but beyond the horizon that has not yet come into view.

One late summer afternoon we went to a favorite place, affectionately called The Acre. We swam in water warm as the air, lazed for a while on the flat granite rock that links the woodland to the water, and were silent. So much else was talking—the wind, the little waves, and an occasional bird. When the wind shifted and the day began to gray toward rain, we went in to the cabin to get a fire going and change back to our clothes. I went down to the lake to fill the very black kettle with water for we were both looking forward to cups of tea.

"When I was a small girl," E.G.V. began, a reminiscent tone in her voice, "I used to sit near my Scottish grandmother, listening to her stories and hemstitching away on a piece of cheesecloth. One night—how is it I recall this so clearly now? perhaps because rain is on the air—a storm was raging outside and my grandmother said to me, 'Eh, sirs, it's a wild night for a soul to be flitting.' I'm not sure that I knew then what she meant, but I did know that we were warm and cozy and safe, but beyond, somewhere, there was a mystery. Perhaps ever since I've been fascinated. The more so the nearer I get to it."

"The Beyond?"

She nodded. "I don't ask questions about it. I'm content to accept, in Wordsworth's wonderful phrase, 'the burden of the mystery.'"

Waiting for the kettle to come to its boil, I thought how lightly time had touched her. Tall, slender, straight, with blue eyes whose color was intensified by the Japanese scarf she was wearing, brown wavy hair done in a classic style with a center part and a knot at the back. Her long legs, always looking longer when she wore slacks, were stretched out to the fire; her hands rested quietly on her lap.

She was one who had walked with sorrow. After less than five years of marriage, when she was barely thirty-one, her husband had been killed in an automobile accident and her own hold on life had been tenuous. Telling me about it once, she said that during the long weeks flat on her back in bed, there had seemed little reason to live without Morgan; but a turning point had come. A realization came over her that he would want her to live and so, for his sake more than her own, she struggled back to life.

For more than forty years she has served in many ways. Early teaching and working for the American Friends Service Committee were followed by the four years in Japan as tutor to the Crown Prince; writing has been continuous in the twenty-five books she has done for young people and adults. And sorrow's grace has been in her availability to others as a source of strength. Dignity is innate with her; discipline is something the years have imposed.

"Perhaps to accept it as a mystery," she picked up the thread of our conversation, "and know that there'll be revelation when we are ready is the key. 'Ripeness is all,' Shakespeare has Edgar say in *King Lear*."

I started to make the tea and commented, "There are certain times in life when acceptance is the only key."

"Yes, indeed. And for me there have been two that I can bring to mind. The first was somewhere in my forties when I had to accept the fact that I was not the writer I had thought I was going to be. The second was somewhere late in my sixties when I realized that my energy was lessening and that time, as we know it, was limited."

"I suppose that second time comes to us all differently, and for different reasons. Often it's no more than a hint, but it shouldn't be shrugged off. The catch is that to most people a horizon is always a long way away."

She shook her head slowly. "I think it's a door; no—let's call it a gate. When I get to it, however my life may be involved, I'll leave whatever I'm doing and go through the gate. It will be natural, inevitable."

"And Morgan will be there?"

"We can't possibly know; our imagination is based on our human experience. But there have been times over the years when I have had a vivid sense of continuing companionship."

Rain had started to fall, but it was a gentle rain, like an accompaniment to our silences.

"What a paradox," she laughed suddenly. "The more you love life and live it, the readier you are for death! I love life—the beauty of the world, the exaltation and daily bread of human love, the joy of work and its fruition, but I look on death as a friend, and it's not the part of a friend to tarry when wanted or needed. Death is a part of life, not an end."

"Reverence for life," I said, "is an idea that has carried with it inspiration, even challenge. Shouldn't reverence for death be more challenging?"

"And the key to that," she lifted her hand in a way that was reminiscent of the teacher in her, "is to live life until we die, right up to the very moment.

"I think that each one of us is given some kind of hidden contract to fulfill with life," she went on. "That may explain why some people don't live out the Biblical span but are taken in the flower of youth and vigor. Perhaps they have done whatever they had to do and are being released for more important work. Life here is such a human venture, I feel that whatever comes after is of a wholly new dimension, unlike anything we can conceive of now. But as love, human love and the love of God, is the highest thing we know of here, I believe that love will be waiting for us beyond the gate of death."

"You and I both know people in nursing homes who are wearying out their days, scarcely alive yet unable to die."

"Perhaps they haven't yet fulfilled their contract. All sorts of important things may be going on within those shells of flesh, for all we know. When I was a young girl I saw a woman who had attained the age of a hundred. There was nothing there but a body—no sight, no hearing, no response. It disturbed me then and the memory does now. I feel we must not let this happen, that we should work on it, tell our deep self that this is not the way we intend to leave life. Work at it now while we are well, as we have been working at much less during the years, and especially at 'our great task of happiness.'"

I could only agree.

"We know that ahead of us lies a certain area of life as real as those we have come through, or are in. It's called old age. We should prepare for it instead of deploring it. Beyond it is another, not an area this time but a step and it is called death. We should make ourselves as ready for it as we would for a journey."

"I'm not sure that I know what you mean when you say 'work at it.'"

"There are some very sensible things we can do, but the most immediate and the simplest is to pray about it."

I felt like a child in the first grade when I said "How?" But it was the only word I could say.

"A few years ago, perhaps taking a cue from Teilhard de Chardin, perhaps because of much visiting in nursing homes, I wrote a prayer for a good death. I say it frequently."

"Will you say it to me?"

"Yes." The rain had eased off, instead of its patter on the roof the only sound was lake water lapping rhythmically at the shore. She began, speaking slowly, thoughtfully: "O God our father, spirit of the universe, I am old in years and in the sight of others. Thou knowest I do not feel old within myself. I have hopes and purposes, things that I still wish to do before I die. A surging of life within me cries Not yet! Not yet! more strongly now than it did ten years ago, perhaps because the nearer approach of death arouses the defensive strength of the instinct to cling to life.

"Help me to loosen, fiber by fiber, the instinctive strings that bind me to the life I know. Infuse me with thy spirit so that I turn to thee, not to the old ropes of habit and thought. Make me poised and free, ready when the intimation comes to go forward eagerly and joyfully into the new phase of life that we call death.

"Help me to bring my work each day to an orderly state so that it will not be a burden for those who must fold it up and put it away when I am gone. Keep me ever aware and ever prepared for the summons.

"If pain comes before the end help me not to fear it or struggle against it but to welcome it as a hastening of the process by which the strings that bind me are untied. Give me joy in awaiting the great change that comes after this life of many changes, let my self be merged in thy Self as a candle's wavering light is caught up into the sun."

She was silent for a long moment, then concluded, "Like all long prayers it is addressed to ourselves as much as to God."

"Amen," I said, "and Amen."

She told me about her most recent visit to England when she had left the friend with whom she was traveling to make a day's solitary pilgrimage to the little church in Norwich where the Lady Julian had been an anchoress.

"When they restored the church of St. Julian after the last war, they found the foundations of the two rooms built against the outer wall where Lady Julian had lived out her life in solitude. They built a little chapel on the foundations. I sat there for a long time. In the cool damp and subdued light, the years fell away and I was back in the fourteenth century. Clearly then, there came into my mind those lovely words of Julian's about the hazel-nut. Remember?"

I nodded, but I could not have said them as she did.

" 'He shewed me a little thing the size of a hazel-nut, lying in my hand; and it was as round as a ball. I looked thereupon with the eye of my understanding, and thought: *What may this be?* And it was answered generally thus: *It is all that is made.* I marvelled how it could last, for it seemed so little it might suddenly have fallen to naught. And I was answered in my understanding: *It lasteth, and ever shall, because God loveth it.* And so the world hath its existence by the love of God.'"

We were both silent. There was much to think about, much to see with the eye of understanding.

"But instead of a hazel-nut, what I saw in my mind was the view the astronauts had when they looked back on the Earth," she said. "All I could think was 'It lasteth, and ever shall, because God loveth it.'"

"My *Juliana of Norwich* is among my beloved books," I said.

"I think, of all the writings of that period, the one I cherish most and reread often is *The Cloud of Unknowing*. It came like sunrise when I needed it greatly, after Morgan's death. It came, stretching long fingers of golden light into the shadows of my mind."

"Books have fed your spirit, haven't they? And mine, too, for you've introduced me to many of your special ones."

"Books and beauty," she said. "This—" and a gesture indicated our little world of The Acre—"and all that's in my memory. Tapestried there. When I'm alone, when I'm waiting for sleep to come at night, when I'm thinking about what I'll be writing, I am aware of beauty—gardens, birds, windy uplands. One time, when I was visiting the Imperial family during the summer holidays in 1947, I stayed at an inn near their villa. In the early morning I was wakened by the sound of hooves and went out on my little balcony. Oh, the beauty of that morning! the tended garden, the pine trees, the mist, the pale pointed mountains against the sky, and the hooves coming ever nearer. Then I saw them as they rode by, two white horses and a bay, the Emperor and his sons, the Crown Prince and his younger brother. They disappeared in the distance, but never from my mind. That picture is always there for me to bring forward and feed myself on."

"Like the 'four ducks on a pond/To remember for years/To remember with tears.' "

"Yes."

We never said to one another, "What are you working on now?" We knew enough about a writer's code, and the total inability to answer that question until the time was right; but we often talked about our work in general terms. She was close to finishing a book; I was close to beginning this one.

"Do you realize how fortunate we are?" she asked. "We're earning our living by doing the thing we most enjoy doing. Doesn't that put us among the lucky ones? Writing has been my life from almost my earliest memory, as it has been yours, and I like the whole process: getting or being visited by an idea, mulling over it for a long time before I begin to put it on paper, doing any necessary research, and at length the writing, the revising, the polishing, sending it off—" She stopped, almost for breath.

"And then waiting."

"Yes, waiting and hoping."

"That's all part of the discipline," I added, well knowing that without discipline, talent, however great, was of little worth.

She turned to face me fully. "And then, something happens, almost before you know it. A new idea emerges and you can hardly wait to get back to your desk!"

"Perhaps we should take those words as a cue," I said, "and get out of the woods while we can still see the path." The dimness of the day had deepened and we were on the edge of twilight.

So we did the few things necessary to leave the cabin in readiness for the next day, then stood on the doorstep for a moment before leaving. Mist was settling. A sighing of wind through the hemlocks caused a spatter of raindrops. When it passed, only the gentle lapping of the water could be heard.

"What a place The Acre is!" she said. "It melts away all one's reserves."

To Make a Plan

LLOYD P. YOUNG

*L*loyd Young and I sat in the room in the house he and Dorothy had planned and help build for their years of retirement. She was not with us, but her work was all around us, weaving especially—wall hangings, cushion covers, and deep tufted rugs. Evidences of their years of travel were there—objects from Peru, from Africa, from the Scandinavian countries, fitting in with the shelves of books that spoke of their academic life, and on the table were periodicals any one of which would have been worth an evening's reading. There were other art evidences, too, in the drawings by the four grandchildren taped on the glass of a door. Looking from the big window, I saw the mountain that dominates our countryside, Monadnock. Steely blue today, its color proclaimed, as surely as the raw wind had, that snow was on the way.

"It's so cozy, this room," I exclaimed, "and the mountain beyond!"

"We planned it that way," he said.

Then, in the orderly manner of a professor teaching a class he knew was interested in the subject, he told me his story of the years. Most of it was "we." Only the first part that led up to his graduation from Emporia State College in 1922 was "I"; for from the time Dorothy Mirth entered his life, up to her death three years ago they were a partnership in everything: their home, their work, their joys and sorrows, their craft.

What a teacher, I thought, as I listened, for he made fascinating the daily events that add up to years; and even as he told me about their life, he was creating a space for me to see mine in some kind of perspective. How he must have helped his students believe in themselves and in the worth of their own ideas!

"When I took my first teaching job out in Kansas, I asked myself what I wanted to be doing in ten years so I could take the first steps. Knowing that I wanted to help others and that teaching was a sure way, I taught for five years. It was during those years that Dorothy and I were married, and the last two years of the five I was made principal of the school; but my goal became school administration. It was William Allen White, that man without an equal, who made his paper, the *Emporia Gazette,* so well known, who helped me set my goal.

"Once, when he returned from a trip east, he

talked with a group of us. I was an undergraduate then. We asked him about the teaching at Harvard, for we were sure it was better than what we were getting at Emporia State. 'The teaching's no different,' he said, 'it's just as good here, but the Harvard students set their goals higher. You can be where you want to be, you can achieve what you want to achieve, and you'll do it by setting your goals high and working toward them.'"

To become a school administrator, a Master's Degree from Columbia University was essential. With just enough money to see them through if they both worked, Lloyd and Dorothy moved to New York. While she put her business skills to use, he studied. On the weekends she typed his dissertation while he did housework. A professor at Columbia put up a five-dollar bet that Lloyd couldn't possibly do what he wanted in the time he had set for himself. When Lloyd received his doctorate in Education Administration, he moved into the future richer by five dollars.

New England had a way of life that appealed to the Youngs—outer ruggedness, inner rewards, and an attitude that linked head and hand in satisfying work. Having grown up in Kansas where the flat land was laid out in squares and where a straight line could be followed, they knew that in New England they might often have to go around a mountain to get where they were going. Lloyd's first years as an administrator were in Holyoke, Massachusetts. In Berlin, New Hampshire, where their two sons were born, he was superintendent of schools for seven years. The next move was to Keene Teachers College as its president, and Keene was home and work for twenty-five years.

During those years much was accomplished and changes were made that would have pleased William Allen White. The college was accredited by the regional and national college associations; a liberal arts program was introduced into the curriculum; the legislature changed Keene's status from a teachers college to a branch of the University of New Hampshire. Lloyd sums up the accomplishments by saying that the greatest of the rewards that came to him was when the students voted to name the new student union in his honor.

Frequently Lloyd and Dorothy asked themselves in the course of those twenty-five years, "What do we want to be doing ten years from now? twenty years from now? Then let's plan for it." Retirement was in their planning.

Dorothy had learned to weave in a class given by the New Hampshire League of Arts and Crafts; Lloyd, called upon so often to help her set up a loom, became a weaver in self defense, or so he says. But he soon found weaving to be challenging and beneficial. Often, on nights when he could not sleep, treadling away on his loom and creating something gave him rest. So, in thinking ahead to retirement, when a home of their own would be possible, a room for their looms was essential.

In the wooded area of Sharon, some twenty miles east of Keene, they bought land and helped with the building of a house that was simple and functional and could not help being beautiful. They lived in it during the summers and went to it for weekends; gradually they cleared land for a far view to the mountain and the near joys of a garden.

Unplanned events enter every life, and when their younger son was killed in an automobile accident, weaving became salvation; especially for Dorothy. The intense concentration demanded, the absorption in devising and then following intricate patterns, helped take her mind from their sorrow.

When retirement came in 1964, they moved into the house they had prepared for their new way of living. Already they were known far beyond New England as master weavers, a husband-wife team who often wore to meetings suits they had made from material they had woven themselves. Now, as they looked ahead another twenty years, they felt that any plans should make room for travel, but travel with a purpose; that purpose would be to see how much they could learn about weaving in other countries and put the knowledge to good account when they returned to Sharon.

A whole sequence of travels followed, to Africa, Sweden, Peru, Greece, Mexico, Guatemala, Ecuador. Some of the trips were made because of Lloyd's work for AID (the Agency for International Development) to help in improving teacher education programs. On these trips, Dorothy could give her full time to studying weaving techniques, but Lloyd never missed a chance to increase his knowledge and skills when time allowed. After each journey they returned to work in their loom room and in their garden, and to catch up with their son's four children. Often they were called on to give exhibitions of their work, and more and more they were drawn into teaching others.

And then one day, returning from a weavers' meeting, their car was crashed into by a reckless driver. People were stunned when the news raced over the countryside and the extent of their injuries became known. Would they ever weave again?

When Lloyd reached this point in the story, I felt close to the experience, for I had gone to see Dorothy in the hospital. Her hands had been the most injured, but his injuries had been the most severe; and while she was in Keene, he was in the intensive care unit of the Mary Hitchcock Hospital at Hanover. While I was with Dorothy, a nurse came in with a note. "They do this every day," she said aside to me. As Dorothy could not hold the paper, it was set down before her on the sheet. It was just three words in shaky handwriting, but they were enough. Lloyd must have said them to her years ago when life spread before them as wide as the Kansas plains. They must have said them often to each other through the years: three words that made love foundation and future.

"It took a long time before we could do much for ourselves again. Dorothy's hands and eyes never came quite right, but the accident stimulated to us to do some things differently and to discover ways that we could help others who had had similar misadventures."

So they picked up the threads as soon as they could, and went on doing what they had been doing and enjoying. "The longer I live," Lloyd said, "the more strongly I believe that service to others is the way of service to one's self."

He took me up a short flight of steps to the large room where they had worked and where he now works alone. Every day, hour after satisfying hour, he sits at one of the many looms, often changing his position to work at a loom of a different size. There is always the mountain to look at when he needs to shift his gaze or rest his eyes, for the whole west wall of the room is glass.

Solidly, Monadnock is there on clear days; just as surely it is there on days of mist or blowing snow.

The looms were of many sizes, large ones for rugs, small ones for belts and scarves, middling ones for lengths of material. All were set up, for he had orders of many kinds to fill and creative ideas of his own for experimentation. There were wools and threads of a gorgeous array of colors and textures, and to many of the looms a pattern that was being followed was attached to the upper part of the frame. Planning was as evident here as it had been throughout his life. Obedient to knowing fingers, the shuttle that passed the woof threads between those of the warp was creating a thing of beauty and, more often than not, of some kind of use.

"I feel Dorothy's influence every day and I keep on doing and enjoying what we had planned for these years."

"And you know—some day . . ."

"Yes." He thought a moment. "I don't know how it will be, but it will be. One cannot have so much for so long and not have it continue in some way."

He had been seventy-seven a few days before my visit. Clear-eyed, straight-standing, with a ready smile and easy speech, he looks like an unusually happy man; but those who know him are aware of a luminous quality which goes beyond the usual concept of happiness. He is doing what he likes to do, has trained himself to do, and he knows that what he does and what he stands for is having an effect on others.

"Some words I heard long ago sum up my feelings now," he said, "as they have through the years. 'The greatest happiness I know is in making other people happy.'"

Looking ahead—as he has done since, as a young man just out of college, he made a plan for the next ten years—my eyes were drawn toward the mountain and my thoughts were drawn to a line from Alexander Pope, something about "the scene of man, A mighty maze! but not without a plan."

A Man with Roots

HENRY ZIBA PERSONS

I sensed vitality when I read about Zee Persons. I was to learn the reason for it in the course of a few hours' conversation and a bowl of lobster stew.

Driving through southern Vermont from the western side of the state, I became aware that I was driving through whole segments of Zee's life and his abiding interests. The sign to Marlboro College reminded me of his long connection with the college and with the Marlboro School of Music. I recalled his words about both, that they were "the yeast needed to leaven the loaf of living" in the hardscrabble life that was much of Vermont. Coming down into Brattleboro, my eye caught the building that was the Vermont Bank and Trust Company. Finding Black Mountain Road, I followed it up and turned on to Kipling Road, and there was the Experiment in International Living with all its flags flying. The mansion, Sandanona, had once been Zee's home. He had always been interested in the Experiment, and after Sandanona became its headquarters his interest intensified.

A mile or so further on was his mailbox and a short piece of road that led to the small house that was now his home. The near fields were green, the distant hills blue. Far to the east I could see the pyramid tip of my mountain, Monadnock, near my home in southern New Hampshire. Breathing it all in, I wondered what this man would be like: banker, philanthropist, philosopher, traveler, friend of people.

Sometimes my courage quails, but there I was on his doorstep, ready to receive what I had asked for—some of his time. There was no going back for me now, even though I might feel hopelessly inadequate before a man who was known in many fields, had done so much in his eighty-three years, and, from what I had been told, was still actively doing.

I pushed the small bell but couldn't hear whether it had rung or not. I hoped I would not have to touch it again; two rings sound so importunate. "Come in," a voice called from somewhere. Pushing the door open, I came and faced a hallway down which a rather short, rather squarish man in a heavy green sweater and baggy pants was coming. He held his arms out to me and all my uncertainty fell away. He didn't take my outstretched hand. He put his arms around me, gave me a hug, and brushed his cheek against mine. It was stubbly. It felt like my father's when I was a little girl and he picked me up and kissed me. I thought, This is one of the bonuses of the years, this getting into a relationship quickly.

"So glad you came," he said, piloting me the rest of the way down the hall and into his study.

There were windows on three sides, each one with a view that lifted the spirit; there was a wall of bookshelves, a table or two with more books, another table with papers spread on it, and there were oddments of many kinds. It was all comfortably untidy, but the sort of clutter that meant many things were being dealt with. I had a feeling that, when needed, he could put his hand on whatever he wanted. He sat down at the desk and I sat near. It was then that I was aware of him—shaggy gray hair and not too much of it, a scant mustache, good color, eyes that gave me confidence. And such a smile!

"I had a wonderful time with you all last night," he said. "I took that walk with you and your dog through Sandwich Notch.* I don't sleep very well and I'm glad that last night I didn't sleep at all; or hardly at all."

He knows me the way I know him, I thought, now we can get on with the business of finding what we think about; and finding something

* *The Road Through Sandwich Notch* by Elizabeth Yates, 1973.

about how to live so one goes on living: not existing, but living.

"I like your sweater, Zee." Everyone calls him that, whether new acquaintance or lifelong friend. It was a handmade, bulky wool, and it looked warm enough for Vermont weather.

"My daughter-in-law made it for me." He ran his hands over it. "I get into it in October and squirm out of it sometime in the spring when the sun starts to warm things up."

The table beside me had two shelves that were crowded with albums. Some looked old, some were recent with maps and travel folders sticking out of them.

He gestured toward them. "If the house should ever catch fire and burn down, those are what I'd save. They're my roots. Family pictures, old letters, a few keepsakes: I'd wrap them around me the way tree roots are wrapped in a burlap bag when a tree leaves the nursery. With them, I could face any kind of transplanting."

"But roots—don't they hold one down?"

"I used to think that, but no more. Take them with you. I want to be mobile. I want to be able to go where life means most, and I can if I have a neat little bundle of strong virile roots that can be tucked down in the earth to grow again."

He leaned back in his chair, the hand that had been gesturing met the other resting on his lap. "Like stories?"

"Oh, yes!"

"Then I'll tell you about Mabel. The story's true, but I've changed her name. You know how that is?"

I nodded.

"Mabel came from a little Midwestern town, and all that goes with it, to New York. She did well in an office, so well that she was soon put in charge and had many people working under her. Now, you've got to remember that Mabel's background had been well established in the little town she'd grown up in. There was never a party without Mabel, never a community effort without Mabel on the committee. When President Harding's train stopped over for ten minutes, her father met him and Mabel was there. Oh yes, her roots had gone deep.

"One day in the New York office a woman who had worked there many years came to Mabel and said, 'How come? After all the years I've been here, it's you who get the promotions, and you're now my boss?' They talked it over in a friendly way because they liked each other, and when Mabel gave her answer it was, 'No matter what comes up, what decision must be made, I feel my own strength. I know that I am Mabel Jenkins of Greenburg, Ohio.'"

He ended with a flourish, using his hands as a conductor might for the concluding chords of a symphony. "See what I mean? Even in her transplanting, Mabel carried the strength of her roots with her. In the new soil they became stronger. Roots don't die in transplanting, they even grow on the way."

I had a feeling that Zee had done more than change a name, that he was really telling me about himself. Perhaps Greenburg, Ohio, was East Aurora, New York, where he had grown up. "You have roots."

"Oh, Lord, yes! Swell roots, strong and sturdy like my grandfather's and my father's." He leveled his glance at me and I saw the twinkle in his eyes. "What do you know about roots?"

"That they're pretty important. If you give me a minute to think, I might come up with a good answer."

"A minute's quite a long time for me to be quiet," he said, and that was the last thing I wanted him to do.

He went on, telling me about his grandfather, who had been a banker, as his father had been, as he had been. Three generations, like the name Henry, but it was going on into the fourth through his son. "A man of integrity, my father, a force in the political life of New York state, and a great one for concentration of responsibility. He used to say, 'Pick a good man and let him do the work, and don't put him on a committee. Committees dilute responsibility and nothing gets done. Beethoven's sonatas weren't written by committees.'"

He moved across the years, making light of his experience—National City Bank, Federal Reserve Board, Reconstruction Finance Corporation; making much of the people he met. "I'm just a social butterfly," he explained, "always have been, always will be. I like people, like to know what they think about, how they feel, and when we get together we talk. Lord, how we talk!

"When I got to be fifty or so, I asked myself what big-city living was all about, crowds and such, like being on a train going like hell downhill, going where you don't want to be. I'd been handling money for years, but I'd learned that it's a god with clay feet, doesn't sustain you the way other things do. I heard of a bank in Vermont that was having trouble—many banks were in those days, the early 1940's—so I came up here to take hold of the bank and live. Everything was so bad, the only thing that could happen was for things to get better. They did, but not soon. I had my desk out front so I could see what was going on, who was coming in. I might be the president, but I didn't want anything to come between me and the people, especially those who needed money, and there were a lot of them."

He shuffled around among the papers on his desk and handed me one. "This was what I asked the tellers to fill out for me when someone came in asking for a loan."

It was pink, about six inches by three, and at the top was printed MEMO TO MR. PERSONS. There were two sections divided by a line. The top one said FACTS, the other one GOSSIP. He pointed to GOSSIP. "That's often more important. I want to know what's been happening—maybe there's been sickness, or family troubles, maybe a prize cow died. Facts speak for themselves. Gossip may hint the real story." He reflected for a moment, then said, "I never lost any money loaning to people, but you had to be sharp when the city fellows came around."

"Your neighbor, Dorothy Canfield Fisher, said that gossip was fiction in the hands of non-professionals."

"Couldn't say it any better, and there's always truth somewhere in the background. But all this is the human side of banking, the personal relations. Today everything's getting away from that. Computers are coming in and when they do the blood oozes out. Automation takes faces off people. Why! I went into the Vermont Bank and Trust the other day to cash a check, and the cute little teller at the first window asked me if I knew anyone or had some identification. And I ran that bank for a dozen years!

"Names are going fast with all these numbers, and as for credit cards! I think they're largely responsible for the inflation we're in. There's nothing right about making people want things they can't pay for."

I must have looked slightly overwhelmed, for

he leaned toward me and smiled comfortingly. "It'd break a snake's back to try to get out of all this, but we're not snakes, and I have a belief that most things work out the way they should. Given time."

We got talking about the appeals that came in increasing numbers for the causes that proliferate. "Many of them go into the wastebasket, as they should. But I like to give where whatever it is, ten dollars or more, will indicate my support of people who are doing a good job. People, mind you, not big computerized organizations."

And then we got talking about retirement.

"I'm something of an expert, you know, and I must believe in it because at the bank I made it mandatory. Fell under my own ax, too, because at sixty-five I was out, the janitor and me. We were the oldest and we had to go, but that's right. Make way for the people coming along. There's no escaping the fact that we slow down with the years. Since I've retired, I've found the way to take longer to do nothing, and sometimes I don't get it done."

Retirement, I thought, remembering his present honorary status on several boards, his work on councils, and even on committees though he looked askance at them.

"But I keep active. It makes me feel good. Here's something—" He rummaged among his papers and handed me the typed pages of a report. It was a study of a garbage project being made by the University of Arizona at Tucson. "You'll be interested in this, because it just may be the fuel of the future."

"Perhaps," I ventured, "retirement well used has something to do with roots."

His eyes that twinkled merrily positively flashed. "You've got it. You know," he said, and his tone went confidential again, "I used to live near a nursery, and I often saw trees being carted out to be planted elsewhere. I didn't feel sorry for them. It looked like adventure to me, and they carried everything they needed in those burlap bags that were wrapped around their roots. Have I told you about my Aunt Susan?"

I shook my head.

"She was one who could say 'I won't' and 'I will' in a voice so uncompromising that I knew it came from her roots."

"Is she in one of the albums?"

"She is, and in me, too. You know, there are some people who get up in the morning, do a day's work, and go to bed wondering why they ever got up. Not Aunt Susan! Not me, Lord, no! There's too much to do, too many people to see, too much to think about. I've got everything worked out with my lawyer, the undertaker, and all that, but I don't know how I'm ever going to be able to take time to die."

"Zee, what about the time you did die in the hospital? What was it like?"

"Well, according to my doctor I was only ninety-eight percent dead, but that's enough to get you across the threshold. It wasn't a place, it was people. Crowds of people, some of them I hadn't seen since I was a little boy. People," he repeated, and fell silent for the space of ten seconds.

People, I thought, they're his life and his roots. They nourish him and he gives nurture to them. I remembered the great redwoods that I had seen in California, but what could not be seen were the roots reaching out and down, entwining with other roots, reaching out and down so a web was made that supported them all. They might bow to the wind and bend to the rain, but they stood. I wasn't surprised that in Zee's case the 2 percent of life brought him back to the people who still were his life.

"Nothing religious about it," he went on, "nothing religious about me. I've always said that all I know about religion is in the Sermon on the Mount and Robert Frost's 'Mending Wall,' but I did send my son to a Quaker school because they're the only people I know who, when a boy falls down, teach him how to get himself up.

"Oh, my mother was religious—always knitting socks for children and reading her Bible. When she got to be ninety, she was content with crossword puzzles, a dictionary, and the Bible. She trimmed down her living to one room, the way roots are trimmed before they're transplanted. 'Blessed be nothing,' she liked to say, and I'm coming to that, too. Witness this snug little house in contrast to Sandanona, where I used to live. But aren't you hungry? You know you were invited to lunch." He looked really concerned.

"Yes, I'm hungry."

"I can give you an option—lobster stew or corned beef hash with a poached egg dropped on it."

"Oh, Zee, what a choice! But lobster is so expensive."

"You forget, I'm a very rich man."

"Yes, of course, a banker must be."

This time his smile said more than words. "I'm rich in other ways. Friends mostly, interests, adventure."

I couldn't put into words what went through my mind and heart, besides he didn't give me time; but it was a long slow surge of admiration for what he was doing in continuing to build human relationships, not for expediency but with genuine love. Solitude might impinge on him, but loneliness would never impede him.

We went downstairs. On the walls were paintings and posters, family pictures, children's drawings: all breathing life and a range of interests. He gestured into one bedroom, then another where his two "guests" lived. The rooms were filled with books—one young man was a student, the other was a teacher. Clothes, ski things, pictures, maps, all proclaimed activity. "I like to have the house used," Zee explained, "and when I'm away they're here to see to things. One of those fellows is a good cook. In fact, he left a cake for us to have for our lunch."

At one end of the long, sunny lower room was a kitchen. The room led out to a garden which looked to me as if, in the season, it must flourish with both flowers and vegetables. Zee soon busied himself around the stove and gestured to the other part of the room that was warmed by an open-door Franklin stove. There were comfortable chairs, deep and much used, and books, magazines, papers. "Sit down and make yourself comfortable. Anywhere. It's all quite clean except for a little dust."

"Can I help you?"

"Nothing to do now this can's open. You can't heat up any better than a stove."

I sat, and started to look at a book. It was about aging, but even before I opened it I felt that Zee could have written a better book.

Soon he joined me, not so much for talk as to put a light on over one of the paintings that took up most of the inside wall. "Now you can walk into it," he said.

Admiring it and becoming a part of it, as one can with an abstract, he started to talk about the summers that were so filled with music. He spoke of Rudolf Serkin. "There's no one to whom I feel closer," he said, "unless it was Pablo Casals. Year after year this house was his when he came to Marlboro for the music festival. One day I watched him practicing with the score before him. It was Beethoven's Second. I'd heard him play it many times and knew that he must have it by heart. 'Maestro, why are you reading the notes? You've played that symphony hundreds of times.' 'Yes,' he agreed with me, 'but last night I missed two notes and I want to find them.' "

Zee returned to the stove and soon called me to sit down at the small round table. He placed a big bowl of lobster stew before me and cut a generous slice from a loaf of French bread.

"I make about eight loaves at a time and freeze them, so I always have bread handy. Like it? There's plenty more."

At some point in the meal I realized that his bowl held bread and milk, not lobster stew. He caught my glance and perhaps my concern.

"The doctor tells me I can eat anything I like, the trouble is I don't like enough to eat. The worst thing is that I've lost my taste for whiskey. However, I'm working on it."

Something in me ached. I knew he was frail, that he had been seriously ill. Probably there was very little he could eat, but that was his affair. He was not going to impose any regimen of his on another; or any problem except to make light of it.

"You know," he said, "for about eighty years I never went into a hospital except to take flowers to a friend who was sick. Would you believe it! I've been in and out of one five times just lately and—"

The phone rang. It was his son in Los Angeles and I heard Zee's end of the conversation.

"Oh, I'm elegant, of course. But can I call you back? . . . I'm having lunch with a charming gal . . . how'd you like a new mother . . . No, I'm going out tonight . . . I'll call you . . . Goodbye."

"Social butterfly!" I exclaimed.

"That's all I am."

The time was moving on and I knew that I should be going. I said as much.

"How soon will you come back?"

"How soon will you be back?"

He ran through his next few weeks. "I'm leaving in a couple of days to be with my son and his family in California for a while, then I want to run over to Tucson and find out more about that garbage project, then—"

"Sounds as if it might be getting toward spring," I suggested.

"And what better time! I'll give you a ring and we'll make a date."

He went with me to the door and we said goodbye. A tender goodbye. As I drove away, facing toward my mountain that peeked over the horizon to the east and putting his mountain behind me, I passed the Experiment in International Living. All the flags were flying gaily in the brisk wind. My gaiety matched theirs, for here was I with a toehold on the future while rooted in spring!

Lao-Tsu put it all in words for me:

> *The man of stamina stays with the root*
> *Below the tapering,*
> *Stays with the fruit*
> *Beyond the flowering:*
> *He has his no and he has his yes.*

Melody of a Life

FRANCES MANN

"I've always wondered what keeps her going," a mutual friend had said to me. I decided to find out.

We had both known her for a long time, known that the mere getting around had never been easy because of a congenital dislocation of her left hip, known that the years had brought other problems —stiffening joints in her hands, cataracts forming over her eyes; yet still she taught her music students and still her burning brightness was undimmed. I made a date to see her and she asked me to spend the night.

Her little house is in Norwich, Vermont, just across the Connecticut River from the spirited life of Dartmouth College in Hanover, and I almost missed it though I had been there before. The evening hour and the last remnants of a winter storm had obscured familiar landmarks, so I went slowly as I approached. But there was the outside light to guide me and the garage door was open; there was the little house, set back from the road and painted such a pale gray that it was almost the color of the snow that had piled up around it. And there was Frances herself, standing in the door, a little more stooped, a little slower in her motions, but with a welcome as ready as ever.

I had forgotten that the house was small when I followed her inside—compact kitchen, bedrooms, bath, all very neat and not so filled with her own things that there was not room for another's. After I had settled in, I went to find her in the living room. No wonder I had carried in memory the thought of the house as large, for this room gave me a feeling of space, space even beyond its walls. At one end a fireplace was flanked by bookshelves, at the other end two grand pianos stood back to back, in between was comfortable furniture and treasures that spoke of travel. A large window looked out across a white field of snow to the rise of a small mountain.

I did not find her in the living-music room but in the kitchen. She was one to whom I might have given the Spanish salutation, "Tell me of your life and your miracles," but she spoke first and asked me about myself.

I told her the reason for my visit.

"You know, I'm seventy-seven."

There would have been no different inflection if she had been telling me she was twenty-one or fifty-three. It was the simple statement of a fact.

But it was more than that for me: it was a door opening two ways with a view down the past and a glimpse into the future. However that might be, the immediate was foremost in her mind.

"If you'll just wait for me in the other room, I'll have supper ready in a few minutes."

Quite clearly there was nothing I could do to help, so I went into the other room that was filled with her life and gave myself a retrospect on her life.

Childhood years had been in Philadelphia, then the family moved to New York. She had come to Vermont in 1964 after retiring from her teaching career. As the youngest of three with two older brothers, one of whom was like a second father, she had been greatly cherished. Her mother sang and Frances accompanied her on the piano, but so skillfully that by the time the little girl was nine years old it was clear that music might well be a major part of her education. At thirteen she entered Juilliard School of Music as a preparatory student. There she went through all the stages that led up to a postgraduate teacher's diploma. From being a student, she became a teacher. Occasionally she gave concert performances in different cities, but teaching was her métier and her joy. She taught at all levels, piano and pedagogy; in time she became Director of the Preparatory Division. Through the years she saw many of her pupils go on to become professional pianists; many more to become accompanists and teachers.

I would have been supremely happy with a bowl of cereal, but not Frances. Supper for her with a guest was steak and all that went with it, ending with bowls of ice cream and lady fingers tucked around the edges. Conversation could attend our meal and continue into the evening. We finished supper just as the clock on the mantel pinged out eight cheerful notes.

"That is, I think, my proudest possession," Frances said, looking toward the clock, "it was given to me by my fellow teachers at Juilliard when I completed my fifty years of teaching."

"But you're still teaching?"

"Oh, yes." She looked at me in surprise. Her face is a very round face and all its features add accentuation—the high cheeks flushed with color, the brown eyes, even the way her white hair is loosely brushed. Her eyes on me were wide with wonder. It was as if I had asked her if she was still breathing.

"Frances, what keeps you going?"

She did not answer immediately and her animated expression gave way to thoughtfulness as if she was searching herself for the answer to my question. When she found it she turned back to me and said with a simple but forthright assurance, "My students."

"Tell me about them." I knew that now she

took only advanced students, or children showing unusual promise.

"It's a wide range," she began, "from five years old up to fifty. If I learn that I can't make them all good musicians, I can make them understanding listeners."

"Within that range, what is the age you like best to work with?"

"Young people in high school, for they can think and reason and absorb. If they are not overemployed in other activities and if they are willing to work, we can go a long way together. Many older students are plagued by self-doubt and fears of performance, especially by memory. All students must, of course, acquire a reliable technique: accuracy, agility, a variety of touches, control and beauty of tone. They should also work on style, form, some chamber music, and as much of the literature as time and industry permit, plus whatever they can grasp of mood and emotional content.

"Sometimes a rare individual comes along, one who cannot do a thing unmusical. When this happens, I know I have real talent to work with."

She told me of a boy who had come to her at the age of eleven, old enough to understand his own physical mechanism as well as gifted with an astonishing ability to project a moving interpretation of everything he studied. After three years Frances felt that the boy would benefit by going to a man teacher. He has since gone on to win high awards in international competitions. "His is an active career as a concert pianist and sensitive chamber musician, and I am very happy about him."

"Isn't it hard for teenagers to put anything ahead of themselves?"

She laughed. "It's often not easy, but it depends on their goals and their standards. Many of my young students prepare to play in competitions to secure scholarships to carry them forward in their careers and they often need a special kind of help. Some will play better with an audience, some will fall apart before one. My days of judging competitions at Juilliard taught me to make allowance for nervous pressures. With all students, confident or apprehensive, there is one touch I try to give and it is the courage to project music through themselves. When they do achieve, no one is happier than I. To see a young person evidence real musicianship, not just a flashy technique, gives me the greatest satisfaction."

Fortunate few, I thought, as I imagined what must take place in that room, Frances at one of the grand pianos facing a student at the other, or if the student was young or timid sitting or standing at his side. For so many young people today, life moves too fast with time evaporating almost before it has gained significance; but here, where teacher and pupil were alone for the space of a lesson, how precious time must become! Metronome or minutes ticking away would have no meaning except as they evidenced mastery of a scale, a phrase, or a complicated cadenza.

I asked if modern trends in music were having any particular effect with teaching.

"Sometimes I feel that I don't understand what modern music is, or what it is trying to say," she answered a little wistfully. "With the early composers, tradition helps: one can sense, can grasp. Take Mozart, there is such freshness and delight in his music, even though his own life was often far from happy. But ask me about modern methods of teaching and I will tell you that we have come a long way. We are freer today, not so rigid, not so tense. Energy that once was confined can now be released."

I had hoped that she would play for me before we said goodnight, but as if she had caught my thought she held her crippled hands out before me. It was the first time I had realized how bent the fingers were, how awkward they must be. I thought of the pain endured, but knew that she would be the last person to speak of it.

"I don't play now," she said, not sadly, not asking for pity, simply stating something that had to be accepted because it was a fact of her present life, as lameness had long been, as her eyes now were. "But sometimes, just for myself, I let my fingers find their way over the keys." She smiled as if to forestall any words of mine and repeated, "Just for myself."

The little clock on the mantel told the hour.

"What note is that?" I asked.

She cocked her head as if to recollect the sound. "I think it is B."

And on that note we said goodnight.

I went down the stairs to my little room where, hours ago, Frances had turned on the electric blanket so I would surely be warm. And, though I did not have music echoing in my mind, I had some words of Siegfried Sassoon's about music:

Beethoven, Bach, Mozart,
Timeless, eternally true,
Heavens that may hold my heart?
Rivers of peace that run beyond the setting sun,
And where all names are one, green Paradise
  apart.

At breakfast the next morning, perhaps because I had gone into sleep thinking of rivers "that run beyond the setting sun," I told Frances of an experience I had had many years ago. It had blessed my life. In the grocery store to make some small purchase, I encountered the owner going about his usual work, yet his wife had died only the day before. She had taught music for many years and was greatly loved. I didn't know what to say to him, but my awkwardness was dispelled when he told me what had taken place in her last few minutes of life.

"She lifted her head from the pillow and listened, then asked me if I could hear it: 'It is so beautiful,' she said. That music was not for me. How could I want to keep her from it?" Ever since, I told Frances, I had felt a wondering expectancy about what is ahead for us all. Something in her expression made me feel free to ask her a question. "Whom would you most like to meet in that land Beyond. Mozart?"

She shook her head and smiled. "A certain student of mine, a mature student. He was gifted, an idealist, a splendid teacher. We did much together, went to concerts, the opera, and shared our thinking. He died some time ago, not at the height of his career but approaching it. I would like to ask him if he is continuing what he began here, if he is finding time to do the things there was never enough time for here, if he is happy. Oh, there would be so much to talk about!"

Even without a reminder from the clock, I was aware that Frances had more than a full day before her. Yesterday's cancellations because of the storm meant that many students would be fitted into today. Her first one was coming in less than an hour; but she was not hurried.

"There is a family in Hanover rich in music," she said, and an undercurrent of excitement ran through the quiet tone of her voice, "the mother is an excellent professional violinist, the two eldest children play piano and viola, the next is a violinist; now, along comes five-year-old Sara whose ear and intuition make her recorder playing quite exceptional. Her mother and teacher think she should start piano and have asked me to take her as a pupil.

"What a challenge for me, with that background, ear and mind! I'm so interested in working with Sara that I told Dr. Charman he must keep me going for another year."

"And then another."

"Yes, indeed, for it will be some time before those hands can span an octave."

When I left, I felt enriched. Here was someone fulfilled at seventy-seven but far from finished, for she had been given another task to do. No music echoed within me as I went on my way but Keats's words had taken on fresh meaning, words about those "unheard melodies" which are sweeter.

"I Make Easy Friends"

ERNEST F. KRONER

*E*rnie speaks nine languages but he has never lost his accent nor his way of changing positions of words in a sentence, and this adds to his charm. Perhaps it was because he does make friends easily that I felt emboldened to ask him if I might talk with him sometime. I knew him only slightly and that from sitting at the same table with him during the past year when he had come on the New Hampshire State Library Commission by appointment of the Governor. Because of his feeling for libraries and his conviction of their influence for good, Ernie had asked to serve on the commission; back of that was a long life's interest in books. From some of our casual conversation, I was aware of the range of his reading and knew that he was a positive night owl when caught up in a book.

I felt he belonged with this gathering of old and new friends who are living with vigor and zest, and savoring each day. We made a date and I would not have changed it for anything, even though the worst kind of late winter storm took over the day we had set aside—snow, rain, sleet, ice, wind, then snow again; and Ernie lives in the White Mountains of New Hampshire where winter can be compounded.

His careful directions led me to the Old Dutch Place, the small farmhouse with a distinctive orange roof which was now barely visible under the new snow. The storm had made me only a little late, and all it did to Ernie was to keep him from the ski slopes and send him instead to an indoor tennis court. *Herzlich Wilkommen* was painted on the door. It opened before I had a chance to knock and the hearty welcome was in Ernie's face, his outstretched hand, his friendly words.

We went into his study to talk. My eye took in quickly the mementos of travel in far parts of the world: the many timepieces, for clock and watch repair had long been one of his skills; the books, the files of film that recorded travels and the different countries in which he has lived, the stamp collection albums. And on his desk the letters both coming and going, for Ernie has friends all over the world and is an inveterate letter writer. But everything was very tidy.

I felt like the King at the trial in *Alice in Wonderland* when he said to the White Rabbit, "Begin at the beginning."

That suited Ernie's orderly mind and was precisely where we did begin.

Born in Karlsruhe, Germany, some years before the turn of the century, Ernie had a much older brother and sister. "I was a latecomer, a Mardi-gras child, but about that I will tell you later." He smiled impishly.

Ernie is a small man with very pink cheeks, thin graying hair, rather pale eyes, and prominent ears. His expression is that of a cheerful gnome and it gave me the feeling that I had met him, or his counterpart, in the illustrations in *Grimm's Fairy Tales*. Quite obviously he enjoys life, and his happiness is enhanced if others are enjoying their lives, too.

"Your rings are handsome, Ernie."

"Oh, yes, I like big rings." He held his hands out before him as if to see what I was seeing. On the third finger of his right hand was a piece of coral in a delicate Chinese gold setting; the left hand carried an opal, iridescent even in a room on a day without sunlight. "The coral I found in Taiwan; the opal my wife gave me when we were in Japan."

During his preschool years, Ernie felt that he was learning almost more about America than his own country, for an aunt who had spent most of her life in the United States had come back to live with the Kroners and play nursemaid to Ernie. Someday he knew that he would go himself to see what his aunt described so glowingly. Caught up in the frenzy of the First World War, Ernie was a flyer at the age of seventeen. He survived four years of combat missions while inwardly convinced that the Allies would be victorious. His friends laughed at him, but he was right. In 1919 he returned to his studies at Technical University in Karlsruhe and graduated with a First in mechanical engineering. Now it was as if the word *Go* had entered his life, particularly since he had become engaged to Else, who had said to him, "Where you go, I go."

In October 1923 they came to the United States. An uncle had found a job opening for Ernie in Auburn, New York. Less than six years later, Ernie and Else received their citizenship papers in the District Court of Cayuga County in Auburn. "On that day of the twenty-fifth May, 1929, I was very happy and proud to call myself an American," Ernie said.

From being an engineer with various industrial companies over several years, Ernie became Chief Engineer and test pilot in an experimental division of the Naval Air Force. During the Second World War he was in Europe again, this time doing intelligence work for the United States in connection with jet aircraft, guided missiles and rocket engines. After these years, and a commission with the rank of Colonel in the USAF, he began work as an industry development advisor with the Department of State Foreign Aid Program.

When Else had agreed to go with him, she

could not have foreseen that such going meant Korea, Japan, many years in Taiwan, and shorter assignments in other South Asian countries. Small wonder that Ernie has acquired nine languages. "For," as he said to me, "how can you with another country deal unless you speak their language?" Spanish is the last language Ernie has studied and that was three years ago in preparation for a visit to South American countries.

A dream of freedom and opportunity held by a little boy had long ago been realized; now another dream that he and Else had entertained could be realized when he retired for the first time from government service; this was in 1960. After searching for years, they found the home they had talked about together: it was in the mountains of northern New Hampshire, in Center Conway. It had stood there for close to two hundred years and had always been known as the Old Dutch Place. Comprising sixty-five acres, more or less, it had a fine trout brook and a sandy beach along the Saco River. There were maple trees to tap for sugar-making. One of them was known to be the biggest maple in the state. Five sap buckets hung from it in March when the sap run began; they built an outdoor fireplace and boiled the sap in the old-fashioned way. They did some farming, but Ernie soon discovered that a man could be good as a mechanical and aeronautical engineer but no good as a farmer.

He shrugged his shoulders and his eyes twinkled as if to say that he who enjoyed jokes could enjoy one on himself.

The only covering on the floor in his study where we were sitting was a tiger skin and I asked Ernie about it.

"Oh," he chuckled, "I shot it in Sumatra, and I feel bad about it now for there are only ten thousand tigers left in the world, but I was staying with a rajah, it was a business trip, and he asked me if I would like to go on a tiger hunt. Of course, I said yes."

Somehow the story of the tiger was not nearly so exciting as the story of the language, Bahasa–Indonesia.

"When that rajah knew I could speak his dialect, he was so happy. I think he would have given me anything, even one of his four wives, but he did give me something very important and that was a clue as to where slate could be found in Indonesia. We had been searching for it for a long time, but always the answer was, 'None there is.' However, after talking with the rajah and discussing terms in his language, he took me to a great source of slate. Good for his people and good for us was the deal that followed.

"No, I would not let the State Department send me to a foreign country until and unless I could speak the language. It's no good working with an interpreter. All the time taken to translate gives the fellow you're dealing with too much time to think what he's going to say to you.

"That is the drawback in this country, too little importance given to languages. Whenever I have a chance to speak to young people, at schools or meetings, I tell them to learn the language of the countries they are going to visit, or may even work in someday. I tell them it is easy!"

Ernie started to explain to me just how easy it was to learn Bahasa–Indonesia and what simple grammar rules it followed. But I could not, even in my wildest dreams, think of an occasion arising when I might find the knowledge of Bahasa useful.

"I'm not going on any tiger hunts, Ernie, really I'm not."

He smiled as if to say, "How can you be so sure?"

Life had been good for many years. Ernie had worked hard to make it so and keep it so, but there came a time ten years ago when Ernie saw no reason to go on living: Else, the dear companion of forty wonderful years, had died.

Religion, as a conventional practice, had not been part of their lives, but from the time the minister in North Conway, a fellow Rotarian, came to talk to Ernie, and continued to come to talk with him, something happened. Ernie began to live again, actively, hopefully. A reunion with Else, in some way completely unexplainable here and now, Ernie felt was based on the scientific view that what has been stored up in the brain over a long lifetime cannot be extinguished by the intrusion of death.

"I do not ask how it will be," he said simply.

Ernie's life now is a continuation of his enjoyment of his friends and his devotion to duty. He mentioned rather lightly the nine voluntary jobs he was doing, among them the State Library Commission, trustee in the Conway Library, president of the Historical Society, the AARP (American Association of Retired Persons), member of the regional stamp club, Rotary district chairman and chairman of the local SCORE (Service Corps of Retired Executives). He plays the *blockflöte* with a group, is a greeter at his church on Sunday mornings, and makes himself available to talk to or with young people. "I can't do much financially for them, but I've had a lot of experience that I can before them lay."

For all his activities, Ernie gives a feeling of inner quiet, or satisfaction; the two are closely related. The discipline of early years added to that of life itself has enabled him to keep both demands and delights in reasonable proportion.

"What gives you the most joy, Ernie?"

"Oh, now you ask me something! It is when I come down the slope of Mount Cranmore on my skis, and I go up pretty high. There is a place where I like to stop, and I do, every time. I look before me and around me and I thank God that I am here, that I can still do this. Yes, that is joy."

"Some people might like to know your secret."

He shrugged his shoulders as if to say that it was only what everyone knew. "I eat three meals a day, not heavy meals but regular meals, and I eat what is good. I exercise every morning as soon as I am up, and I exercise at night before I go to bed. But don't think it is easy. Sometimes it is hard, very hard."

He stopped, but I knew he had more to say.

"It was some years ago that my doctor friend said to me, 'Never give up, Ernie; when you give up you are finished.'"

It was not entirely the exercises and the physical activity that the doctor meant, of that I felt sure.

"Maybe it is good to be a Mardi-gras child." His eyes twinkled as he spoke.

"Oh, Ernie, you said you'd tell me what that means," I reminded him.

"Please," he said smiling, "excuse for me that I take so long to come to this the first part of the story." A smile comes readily to Ernie's face and this time it spread from ear to ear.

Then he was off on a tale that has no parallel in our land. Not that there are not "accidents," but none under such hilarious circumstances.

"In days gone by, Mardi Gras was a time of celebration, *Fastnachtdienst,* and it lasted for three days," Ernie began. "Everybody was masqueraded, even some real old people. All females were allowed to be kissed by menfolks. During these days people ate what were called *Fastnachtskuechle,* doughnuts without holes in them. In our house there was always a big laundry basket full of these doughnuts and a big pot of coffee on the kitchen stove. There were parades with floats and musical bands—military bands, workers' bands, bakers, butchers, plumbers, and all were masqueraded; even the horses were masqueraded. There were carnival balls at night and always a real big one in the city's convention hall with thousands of people dancing and frolicking all night. In every town or city there was a Prince Carnival's headquarters in a hotel-restaurant, with masqueraded guards and guardhouses in front."

Ernie gave me time to let this marvelous picture sink into my mind, then he smiled slyly. "In my old home, our neighbors on either side were a butcher shop and a grocery store. The butcher's Mardi-gras child was thirteen years younger than the next of his five brothers and sisters, the grocer's was nineteen years younger. Now, you know what I mean when I tell you that I am a Mardi-gras child."

He had scarcely finished when we were called to tea. We went from the study to a small dining room near the kitchen, but we might have crossed the ocean and all the intervening miles, for we were in Germany: the furniture was of golden-toned larchwood with typical Black Forest carvings; overhead was a gaily painted and carved wooden chandelier with peasant musicians. There was a corner clock. A large window looked out on the white and wintry world, but I saw it through squares of stained glass and the snow took on rainbow hues. We had tea and a German crumbcake and went on talking.

On my way home I felt as if I had opened a book and read only a few pages in it. There was so much more I wanted to read, and would on another day. Ernie had called the time "a happy and dazzling serenity." He who could be easy with many languages had chosen his English words with care.

"You Don't Think I'm Going to Sit Down, Do You?"

ISABELLE ANDREWS BUCHANAN

*I*t was a chance meeting, but it was only the beginning. An acquaintance of mine, driving down our road one day, saw me working in the garden and stopped to say hello. With her was her aunt, a Mrs. Buchanan. Though the visit was brief I knew that some day soon I wanted to know Mrs. Buchanan better. A few months later we made a date and I went up to spend an hour with her at her home in Concord, New Hampshire.

She is the sort of person you would scarcely notice if you saw her on the street or in a store or on a bus, and if you did you might think, "What a spry little lady she is, the kind one sees often in New England." And then you might wonder why New England is rich with such people. Has it something to do with standing up to the capricious weather—summer heat, winter cold, the unexpected, and the change that caused Mark Twain to comment, "If you don't like the weather, wait a minute"? People have a way of making their own weather, and what drew me to Mrs. Buchanan was a feeling that, tiny as she was and old as she must be, she was meeting life on her own terms.

Promptly at three o'clock I rang her doorbell. It was soon answered and her welcome was immediate. She looked smart in a two-piece buff-colored suit with a wide white collar that set off her face. Her trim figure gave no hint of the hump between her shoulders until she turned. Her gray-white hair, brushed high, gave her height. The way she said my name, the strength with which she clasped my hand, made me feel that I was in for a happy time.

We sat down in a small comfortable room filled with evidences of the years—family pictures, little treasures and keepsakes, an African violet with more blossoms than leaves, the daily paper, a Bible that looked much used. I admired some petit point, a chair seat that was nearly finished. She picked it up, handling it pridefully, and said, "It's hard to get time to do all the things I want to do, but I love them, all of them."

After an hour's talk, and during it, I realized that was the key: she loved everything she did, everyone she met.

As the youngest in a farming family in the mid-1890's when livestock and crops were a solid part of the economy of New Hampshire, she admired her elder sister but she was the pet of her three elder brothers. They took her everywhere with them and let her do everything they did. She grew up with as companionable a feeling for horses and cows and sheep and chickens as she did for the people around her. If she was her brothers' pet, she must have been her parents' joy. She helped her father wherever she could and followed her mother around doing everything she did in house and kitchen, dairy and garden. The little girl took pride in the tasks given her and felt privileged.

By the time she could hold a darning-egg in her hands she started to earn her own money. A penny a sock was the going rate, and when enough pennies piled up she took five to buy an ice-cream cone at the store. Allowed to dust for a neighbor, her wage was generally a large piece of cake which she took home and divided with her family. It was idyllic, growing up at a time when life moved slowly and the family circle was its boundary. Days were long and love was sure.

The pattern changed the day the ox team was transporting a last load of cordwood. The load tipped and Mr. Andrews went under it. He survived, but not to walk again around the farm he loved or the nearby estate he managed.

The elder sister was married, the brothers were in college. Isabelle started to hoard the pennies she earned toward the time when she, too, could go to college. At fourteen she was old enough to wait on table at a summer hotel. In between she helped her mother, who now took in summer boarders. She took in laundry too, and Isabelle helped with the ironing; it gave her time to dream about college. Domestic science and nursing were skills she hungered to improve, having done much of one and being called on to help with the other.

When school was finished, she was forced to face a new fact that college could not be for her. The tension of life with little ready money, the increasing needs of her invalid father, meant that there were no funds for her further education; even her savings were not enough to help. The disappointment was so overwhelming that it resulted in a nervous breakdown, and for close to a year the once eager girl was of little help to others and none to herself. Then something happened. Seeing with sudden clarity that if she was ever to amount to anything she would have to rely on herself, she took hold of her life. From then on she knew that nothing would get her down again.

College was only temporarily out of the picture, she told herself. A year or two at the most and the Andrews family would catch up with events and she would be able to follow her dream.

She tried for a job in the nearby telephone exchange. Out of fifteen girls tested for the quality of their voices, she was one of two who met the test. Whether she knew Shakespeare or not, she was living up to the lines in *King Lear,* "Her voice was ever soft,/Gentle and low, an excellent thing in woman." She could be heard and understood, and she could listen. She loved the work, especially when there were personal calls to be relayed. The reporting of an accident was exciting, as was a fire when help was needed speedily. Three years in the exchange saw a tidy sum accumulating and the dream of college came close to reality.

Then one winter's day, hurrying to do an errand, she slipped on the ice. It was a serious fall, resulting in a curvature of the spine that would give her a visible burden to carry the rest of her life. All the money she had saved went to pay the doctors' bills. After six months flat on her back, she learned to walk by pushing a chair before her. "If I can ever walk again," she told her father, "I will never complain." The statement became a maxim by which she lived.

And college? A family friend said to her, "If you study and observe, you'll get as good an education in time as if you went to college." She might not be ready to agree, but she had to accept the fact, hard as it was. Vicissitude was a word whose meaning she did not learn from a dictionary but from life itself.

At her father's death the house and farm were sold and all the contents auctioned. A few cherished pieces were saved—a spool bed, a small table, her doll, some books. It was hardly enough to warrant a load when she and her mother hitched the old horse Harry to the buggy and drove from Sutton down to Concord to live. They were not alone for long. She was twenty-eight when, from being an aunt, she became a mother of three. Her sister and her sister's husband died within eleven weeks of each other and their children became members of the household which Isabelle and her mother had set up.

"You don't think I'm going to sit down, do you?" became a familiar phrase.

She could cook and clean and nurse and care for a family, but there would be need for actual money if they were to be well educated. She saw a possibility in merchandising. A large department store in Concord could use a salesperson on the "intimate apparel" floor. She got the job and soon learned that the real money was in corsets. So she went to New York to study their proper fitting. When she returned—and for the next forty years—she had as much pleasure working with the figure as an artist would.

"That was in 1920," she explained carefully while her face crinkled with the smile that was a part of every story, "and the controlled figure was in vogue. Were it today, I'd have had to find another job."

We both agreed that today's natural lines were

better, especially when women exercised their own control and did not rely on whalebone.

"My father could estimate the weight of a cow or a sheep just by looking at it and I could estimate what our needs would be if those children were to have the right start in life. It wasn't long before I knew that I must have a raise. Oh, not for myself! I had a blue dress and a black dress that I wore with collars and cuffs, different ones that I changed every day; and I had always been able to set aside something for my church. But I had to look ahead, so I went into Mr. Emmonds' office one morning and I knew that I wouldn't leave until I got my raise." The mobility of her face accented her every word.

"I told him that since I had taken over the department the business had grown one hundred percent. He had to agree because it was true, but his eyes went right through me while I stood there and he gave me every kind of reason why a raise was not possible. I said to him as clearly as I knew how that I wasn't asking for any one-dollar or two-dollar raise, but for a five-dollar one." Her eyes flashed as she relived the scene.

"Well, I got it." She was like an orchestra conductor terminating a surge of sound with the swift movement that brought silence.

I was speechless, awed by the bravery of this one small woman who had dared Big Business and compelled from its representative a (then!) living wage of thirty-five dollars a week.

"Oh, I loved my work and the people I worked with, and I loved seeing the children grow up and get ready to take their places in the world." A rather special expression came over her face and I knew that she was about to share with me another rare moment in her life. "I was sixty-two when I got married. Think of that!"

Some friends of hers arranged a social engagement with Stanley Buchanan, a widower with two grown sons. Acquaintance culminated in a proposal of marriage, but Isabelle Andrews thought for a year before she gave her consent.

"I was fond of him," she went on, "almost from the start, but I had to be sure it was the right thing to do. I always think clearest when I waken early and one morning, about three o'clock, I went over the step in my mind, estimating it from every angle I could think of, and I decided it was right. So, we were married. And I loved it! We had a good many years together, too. I'm alone now, have been for quite a while, but there's so much to do that I find the days aren't long enough.

"And as for that piece of petit point," she gestured to where she had laid it down at the start of our conversation, "I hope soon to find time to finish it."

"Tell me some of the things you do."

"Well, for one, I love to call on elderly people and take them out for drives. I have a particular friend, she'll be eighty-nine this month, who enjoys fried chicken, so that's what we get when we go out. One of my boys—my stepsons—comes around often to see that my car is in good condition, and I don't ask too much of it. Then I love to call on the sick, to bring them little things, you know. Church work takes a certain amount of my time, always has, and then there's the garden club, and cooking for friends who don't do much of that any more, and I do love to have a friend in for luncheon now and then."

Near where we sat was a "perpetual motion" clock with a pendulum that went round and round. She told me that it needed to be wound only once a year. Looking at it, I was aware that my hour had gone. As the clock was running a bit slow, I had probably overstayed my time; so I began to say goodbye.

"But you can't go until you've had tea!" she exclaimed. "And I've got everything ready." Leaving me, she went down the short hallway to the kitchen, her steps as precise as her words. "I do love tea, don't you?" she called to me.

"Yes," I said, realizing how many times she used the verb *love*. And it had not been lightly used at any time, for Isabelle Buchanan loved life and all that it brought to her.

Reflecting on some of our conversation while she was busy in the kitchen, I decided that she had discovered and was utilizing three rules good for any age but especially good for the eighties:

she did everything in the easiest possible way, she took frequent rests, and she gave herself little indulgences. In telling me about her housekeeping, she explained that she did it a little at a time and never let things pile up so there was more than she could handle comfortably. Evidently she had learned to recognize the body's signals, because she rested willingly, lying down with a book or her thoughts and letting energy flow back again. And she did relish that occasional cup of tea; a demure indulgence it might be, but it was restorative.

Returning, she poured the tea into delicate cups. "It always tastes better out of real china, don't you think?"

I agreed.

She offered me some cookies she had made that morning. "I'll give you the recipe before you leave," she said. "It's a new one to me and I think they came out well. When you get around to it, help yourself to those date-and-nut squares. I made an extra lot for a friend who can't get out any more. I'll put up a little packet of them for you to take home."

When I left, I almost expected to hear old Harry whinny at the hitching-post, for I had been in his world for a time and was reluctant to move back into mine. "But if she can merge the best of the past with the pressure of the present with such *élan*, I can too," I told myself.

Whether the day was sunny or rainy, hot or cold, was then of little concern to me: I had been with someone who, from the time she took hold of her life to manage it, had made her own weather.

"I Want to Help"

EDWARD S. BOOTE

*H*ow, and to whom, does one tell a dream? Not to everyone, and only when a climate of sympathy exists. But there are some rare ones in this world with whom this climate always exists. Such are the Bootes.

And my dream.

Perhaps because of early influences. One was a teacher so physically frail with age that there was something transparent about her but with a mind that scaled Olympus and in converse with the gods brought them down to my eight-year-old level. I wasn't much older when she died. It was my first experience with death and it was filled with light. I felt that now her converse with the Lofty Ones could be made more easily. Another was a farm woman in whose kitchen I sat by the hour listening to her stories, helping her to make bread and to preserve the summer's harvest of fruit. And there were others. With them I felt safe; their quiet gave me the feeling that their concern was with the things that deeply mattered. With them I sensed something of the bourne toward which all life tends. Sometime, some way, I hoped to repay a debt to the dear ones who had so enriched my childhood.

In 1941, when Bill and I made our home in southern New Hampshire, we found the perfect place for our roots. It was an old farm with a brook and a view of mountains; a third of its sixty-seven acres was open land, the rest was wooded. The house was small and sturdy, built in the late 1700's; there was a stalwart barn, a carriage shed, a milk house.

Restoration revealed lovely features, and during the years everything had its use. The carriage shed was made into a guest house, the other small building became Bill's office. The fields were leased to a farmer; the forest gave us cordwood and trails for walking and snowshoeing. The land near the house responded well to gardens for flowers and fruit and vegetables. We called it *Shieling*, a word we had come upon often in the highlands of Scotland, meaning "a little house in a clearing," "a shelter from the weather." A mile from the town as Shieling is, in an area culturally rich, there seemed so much that was so right. For these many years, Shieling has been all that a home can be to those who live in it, to those who come to it. One day a friend said, "Shieling is a family," and from that time on all who were part of our life became our family.

I am alone now, but these loved acres, these lived-in buildings are my care, my dear care. Could it be that I might make of them a community for older people, people who want to live simply with some responsibilities taken from them so their time can be given to growing inwardly and their special interests can be more easily pursued?

The field that reaches from the garden to a pine-clad slope could accommodate some twenty small dwellings for perhaps twice that number of people. Each would have its own garden space, its mountain view, its cozy compact living. Comfort, safety, beauty would all be part of the design. These words kept running through my mind: "simplicity, economy, ease of operation"; wrapping them up was another word, "community." In time the house would be used as guest rooms, library, office; the barn would be a gathering place, perhaps a refectory. The dream named itself Shieling Home Place, the last two words those that have long been used in New England parlance to designate the land near house and barn. I began to talk to people about it; it began to seem real.

One winter afternoon, having tea by the fire with two friends who were ready to move in as soon as the first little house was built, one of them said, "You should talk with Ted Boote."

"But I don't know Mr. Boote, just his house."

Some six years ago, I was aware that Mr. and Mrs. Edward S. Boote had come to live in Peterborough. Leaving four out of their five acres untouched, they built a house on land that had once been a pasture where Guernsey cows grazed and where I had often found wild strawberries. Other houses were being built in the pasture and, much as I had loved the Guernseys, I knew that land so near the town could not remain rural. I was happy that the people who were building there showed their feeling for the land in the way they were setting out trees and establishing gardens. Especially the Bootes. Their house was low and traditional, white with dark green shutters, a big center chimney, a small lawn and a garden that was mostly wildflowers. I used to walk by it in the evening and wonder what they were like. Their names appeared in the local paper now and then and I knew that they identified themselves with the town in many worthy ways.

"How could I meet the Bootes?" I asked.

"We can arrange that easily."

So, having known the Bootes' house for five years, within that many days I knew them. Mutual friends brought them in for an afternoon of talk and tea. Too much friendship time had already gone by, but I had the comforting feeling that we would know each other for the rest of our lives. Soon I was telling them about my dream. They listened with a quiet intensity that I was to learn was characteristic of them both. Every now and then Ted would say, "I have a question," and in answer I gave a fuller description of some aspect of Shieling Home Place.

I could feel Ted's mind working as his questions came and my answers followed. I could feel my mind expanding as I was queried and compelled to consider matters I had not really faced up to. What was the funding? How about a board of directors? These, and much else, were details that had not challenged me greatly, and yet I saw that in facing them my dream would be given a foundation. Only with that could it grow.

As we talked, Anne listened. There was a look in her eyes as if she was seeing beyond the beginning to the completion. And so she was; for when she spoke it was of the landscaping—the way flowers and vegetable gardens would come into the picture, lilacs and blueberry bushes, native shrubs and wildflowers. There was a light in her face that was a reflection of her vision. She began to explain how she hoped it could be developed if she might play some part in Shieling Home Place.

If I have learned anything, it is that when an offer is made acceptance is in order, so I exclaimed, "We'll turn the landscaping over to you!"

Her eyes shone.

"She's the one who can do it," Ted said. There

was a courtliness in his words that made me feel he was bowing with admiration to her skill.

How blessed am I, was my only thought: green-fingered Anne and business-minded Ted were now part of something that was rapidly becoming "a project."

At the door when we said goodbye, I happened to mention that Shieling was close to two hundred years old.

"And I'm going to try hard to see my third century," Ted announced.

I paid little attention to the remark then, but it lodged in my mind. I knew that I wanted to talk with him about himself and about what kept him forward-looking at a time when some people tend to look back.

So, on an April evening when snow had gone but warmth had not yet come, I walked the short half-mile to spend an hour with the Bootes. There was no moon, but I had no need of one to guide me. Herbert Trench's lovely line moved through my mind, "By starlight and by candlelight and dreamlight." As I approached the house I saw daffodils glowing in the light that came from the windows.

Ted opened the door, Anne stood near. "I'm glad you walk when you come to see us. It's such a friendly thing to do," he said.

In a small sitting room we sat and talked. Evidences of their lives were there: of Anne's in a pot of polyanthus on the table, fragrant and an unusual color—not yellow or orange but a blend of both—a chair covered with her needlepoint, a small pillow with her crewel work, for her fingers had the skill to make beauty bloom with silks and threads as well as with flowers; and of Ted's in bone china figurines that spoke of his English forebears, a painting of grouse flushing over pointing dogs on an autumn hillside from the years when he had been an upland-game and bird-dog man, and weather gauges in a corner with their immediate information.

If Ted's familiar phrase was "I have a question," mine might well be "I want a story." And I was to have it. With only a query or two from me, Ted told me about his life, beginning methodically with his birth in New Jersey in 1898, and his moving into the world through college days and after; at the point where Anne and her three children entered, the story became their life.

He sat relaxed in his chair, a big man with shoulders that are always erect, a clean-cut profile, thin sandy hair and eyes to match, a pale face kind and quiet. Whether he speaks, and his words are well chosen as if he thought them first, or is silent, he has an air of nobility. Trying to describe him to myself as he talked, I kept coming back to Chaucer's knight in the Morrison translation which I had recently been reading, one who "loved chivalry,/Truth, open-handedness, and courtesy."

"The first book I was ever aware of," Ted said, "and I remember it well today, was a geography. I was a very little boy, but it made me want to see the world, to know the world, and to escape into it from the darkness of life that was my home."

As he told me the story, it was hard to believe that his late childhood and early teens had been a dismal passage of time from which he yearned to be free. The long illness of his mother; later his revered father's remarriage which brought him a step-brother near his age in the pre-teens, but nowhere near in compatibility. Much as he loved his father, love stopped there. Ted looked ahead to the time when he would be his own man. His four years at Wesleyan University gave him the joy of independence. He was an honor student and head of student government; he also received honorable mention as the leading drop-kicker in Eastern collegiate football in 1919, and captained the Wesleyan baseball team.

Anne, listening as I was, came in with the remark, "Those were the happiest years of his life."

Ted looked at her. "No, dear. The happiest years were after I met you."

He had met her in 1926 but their lives had gone separate ways and he saw little of her again until the 1940's. When they were married in 1948 life took on a different hue. I thought to myself, "The early years may have been dark but he's had thirty years of happiness, years that will stretch into eternity. That's more than many people have or could hope for." Meanwhile Anne's two sons and her daughter have been blessed with a total of twelve fine children, a constant joy to both their grandmother and to Ted.

Ted went from the room for a moment and came back with a paper in his hands. He explained that the friends of William Day Leonard, an alumnus of Wesleyan, class of 1878, had set up in 1917 a scholarship fund in his memory. It was an award to be made annually at commencement. Ted started to read from the paper, " 'To a member of the Freshman, Sophomore or Junior Class and to be used against tuition charge at the College for the ensuing year. Three men to be nominated by members of the Senior Class who are members of the College Senate, this selection to be made on the basis of the characterization of a man used by Leonard himself.' " Ted looked at me over the edge of the paper, "It's impossible, but this is it." He read from the page, " 'Accomplished without ostentation, grave without austerity, gentle without weakness, cheerful without frivolity, conciliatory but not unbending, rigid in performance yet indulgent toward all faults but his own.' "

I gasped, "But that's a description of you!"

"From the three nominated, the faculty were

to select the man for the award," Ted said as he folded the paper and put it in his pocket. "The award was given to me in 1919, my junior year. It was the first time it had ever been given. It has been given every year since then."

Anne and I exchanged glances. I guessed that our thoughts were running along the same lines.

"It was an honor to receive it," Ted went on, "but more than anything it gave me confidence not only for my senior year but into life, and confidence was what I needed more than anything else."

After college in 1921, Ted learned that the Ludlow Manufacturing Associates, headquartered in Ludlow, Massachusetts, needed a few young men as staff for their newly constructed jute mill near Calcutta, India. He applied, and was accepted for service in the subcontinent, where most of the world's jute fiber is grown. He felt he would have to learn everything he could about jute in order to serve the company well as their jute buyer, which, even then, he aspired to become. His persistent desire to know the answers to his questions combined with his childhood desire to know the world: that never-to-be-forgotten geography book had much to do with launching Ted in his business career. He spent a total of six years in India, four consecutively in the early 1920's, hard-working, enriching years that exacted a cost. Falling prey to most of the calamitous diseases in that disease-ridden land, he was invalided home; but the Ludlow company never lost touch with him. Well again, Ted was offered an executive position which he kept for enough years to add up to a total of nearly sixty. Jute was his business life, but service to his fellows kept pace as he responded to demands which challenged and broadened his concept of social responsibility.

Because of India, Kipling's books are his favorite secular reading; because of the long influence of his two grandfathers—one a Methodist bishop, the other a strict Presbyterian in whose home Ted was brought up until his father remarried—the King James Bible is the book on his bedside table. "It gives us the answers to our questions," Ted commented, "if we're willing to think about what it says to us."

And because of those early discordant years, harmony is his mainspring. He has found it in his home, he achieves it in his relations with others, he has it in music. With no formal training but with an infallible ear, he plays several instruments. In college it was a mandolin, now it is an autoharp; all along it has been the piano. He sang in the Wesleyan a cappella quartet when in college, and now sings with a choral group and in the choir of his church.

The edge of eighty is not reached without some reminders that the body is not a permanent habitation. Ted's eyes are helped by glasses, his ears with a hearing aid. During the past ten years he has been twice immobilized as first one hip joint then the other has been replaced with metal and plastic. He sometimes walks with a cane, but gracefully. Hanging by its crook from one of his pockets when not in use, it looks as inconsequential as a pair of gloves.

His philosophy is so simple that he feels it scarcely bears repeating. "I'm happiest when doing something for someone else, someone I love, or a neighbor." With his words there was a slight but courtly inclination of the head first to Anne, then to me. "That is the best," he said, "but it could be anyone."

A few years ago the century-old country church in which he sings on Sunday mornings decided to replace its electric organ with a pipe organ. Ted headed the committee for the replacement. Thorough in everything he does, he and the committee extensively traveled to hear and discuss the various types of organs available. When the pipe organ was chosen, a professional study of the church structure was arranged, and the organ was installed in a position that avoided any possible damage to the ancient structure. With the organ in regular use, Ted, as trustee in charge of maintenance, periodically inspects the instrument. These visits also give him an opportunity to sit down at the organ for a time of peaceful relaxation and to hear tones of a richness and harmony almost unbelievable to one whose experience has been solely with the piano. "It's really hard to leave the organ," he says, "after having played some of my favorite hymns—such as Whittier's 'Dear Lord and Father of Mankind,' and others that combine heavenly thoughts and glorious harmony.

"There are so many things we can't explain," he went on as if his thoughts had been otherwhere. "And there is much we know without explanation." His gaze rested on the polyanthus on the table, glowing in its saffron-hued bloom. "Nothing but a power above ourselves could do that, and that's enough for me now." His tone changed, becoming brisk and efficient. "But we've had enough about me, how about you and what's the latest news on the Home Place?"

I, too, had been otherwhere and could not bring myself immediately to practical matters. Ted sensed my hesitation in shifting subjects, and helped me through it.

"The things that happen as one gets on in years," he said gently, "the little disabilities, the big difficulties, tend to make one lose confidence, but this plan of yours is giving me something, the way the Leonard Award did sixty years ago."

It pleased me that he called it a plan. I told him about a recent meeting with the attorney, about the plot study the surveyor was making, about the architect's sketches we would soon be examining. "There's much to do, but every move is a step in the right direction."

Ted's response was typical: "I want to help you all I can."

My hour had long gone and I got up to leave. Ted went to his room and came back with the big volume of Kipling's poems. Reading aloud as we went toward the door, I felt that I was being ushered out with flags flying and martial music. He wanted to drive me home, but I wanted to walk. That short half-mile would not be long enough for all I had to think about. By starlight then, and dreamlight, I went on my way, assuring myself that there are some to whom a dream can be told and there is a time for the telling.

The Balanced Equation

ROBERT C. CHARMAN, M.D.

*W*ith regard to time, Robert Charman does not have a place in these conversations for he has scarcely moved into the second half of life; with regard to understanding what I have been seeking, he has his place. There were some matters that I wanted to clarify from a medical point of view and I valued his approach.

I'm curious. It's a writer's motivation, and over the years I've learned where to find the answers to some of my questions—in libraries, from authorities, through long thinking. "Curiosity killed the cat," but it makes the writer. With anything that intrigues my mind, I want to know how it happened and why, and what resulted. I have the same curiosity about life, the process that's been going on in me since I got into the world and that's been all around me since the world began. Call it growth based on universal laws. We can't hurry it any more than we can delay it.

There were, quite naturally, a good many years when I did not think of this process; but now the years are adding up and I find that I am thinking about it increasingly. Time that once seemed forever now has limits, and within those limits are elements to be discovered, for time is the raw material with which work is done and I can no longer be spendthrift of it.

Philosophically I tell myself that life isn't so much a being as it is a becoming, and that what is really going on in me is preparation for another kind of life. But it is good to balance the philosophical with the practical, and there were questions that a doctor could best answer. So I met with Dr. Charman in his office at the Hitchcock Clinic in Hanover, New Hampshire.

"Why do some people go on functioning regardless of calendar age, and some do not?" I asked.

"You've been finding an answer to that one with your conversations," he replied. "I think the aging process is possibly slowed up or meliorated for people who have a sense of purpose."

"Well then, how can we all make the living of our lives as physically good as possible"—I halted, wondering if I could say what I wanted to say—"and as spiritually sound?"

The slight nod he gave made me feel that we stood on the same ground.

We talked about rules of health that are so simple, sensible, and rewarding that one wonders why they are disregarded so cavalierly. We talked about problems compounded by time, and about emergencies such as coronaries and strokes. We talked about the way the heavy hand of illness and woe is laid indiscriminately.

"A normal good diet with plenty of vegetables, fruits, and whole grains, especially from the seventies on, is the only sensible one," he said. "Most people in this country eat too much meat, too many fats, too much sugar. Many people do not exercise enough; but it's fully as important to recognize the need for rest, occasionally throughout the day to recharge the batteries. To be alone at times is good therapy and, in line with that, the practice of meditation so popular with young people today is effective, especially in cases of hypertension. A physical check-up now and then, particularly for people over forty, is the best prophylactic."

I was interested to hear what he would say about situations where the mind seems to deteriorate while the body goes on. To this he had no easy answer except to say that it is something medical research is working on.

"Of the people you see daily and treat constantly," I asked, "how many physical conditions are influenced by mental attitudes?"

"All of them," he replied without hesitation. "I try to understand what the mental or spiritual problem is. It helps to know, but it can't always be found. Some people give up easily, some battle on. In many cases, gallant certainty of spirit can tip the scale in favor of recovery."

Leaving his office, I went on with my pondering; but I felt a kind of support from all that he had said.

It's reasonable to assume that we had nothing to do with our getting into the world but, once here and conscious of the fact that we are individuals in control of our own lives, it's fully as reasonable to tell ourselves that we have a great deal to do with how we get through the world and eventually out of it, with style and even bravado.

I thought of some of the problems imposed by the aging process, obvious ones to be seen as the attrition of the years and to be helped with mechanical means like glasses, hearing aids, walkers. I balance them with the riches of the years. Marvelous to me it is that things don't hurt the way they once did. It is as if an immunity to one's own suffering had been building, while compassion for others' suffering had been deepening. Selectivity has been growing; more and more it is only the real things that matter. Perhaps this has something to do with perspective. There is a need for quiet, both inner and outer, and with the need a willingness to accept repose.

Creativity is rarely impaired by time. This may have something to do with the fact that the creative person has submitted from the first to the discipline of craft or profession, and discipline is implicit with life well lived. Alice Keliher, noted educator and long-time friend of mine, said to me recently, "If you are absolutely convinced of what you believe in, and have no internal tug-of-war, age is of no account." Beginning with John Dewey, she cited a number of people in her own field as well as in other fields who have lived productively far beyond the Biblical three score years and ten.

It takes imagination as well as determination to maintain good physical condition, to make new friends as old ones slip away, and to keep the sights ahead. It takes a firm hand to simplify living, to keep demands in control, and get out from under the burden of too many things, for accumulation and cumber impede resiliency. Each one of us has just so much energy, and the supply is less renewable as the years go on. To see the work to be done and to conserve energy so it may be done is to go a long way into fulfillment.

It was like Dr. Charman to follow our talk with a letter.

"I've had an opportunity to ponder some of the points discussed during your visit," he wrote. "I suspect a major reason for the productivity of some people is an appropriate stimulus balanced against a fertile mind. By 'appropriate' I mean the stimulus can neither be overwhelming nor meager. For some people it may become more than an incitement to activity; it may become a challenge. If it is accepted and if the challenge is not too great, much meaningful productivity can ensue.

"The other half of the equation is the mind and character upon which the stimulus acts. This is the unknown part of the equation. From whence comes the creativity, the determination, the self-reliance, and the 'guts'? In order for the equation to work it clearly must be a balanced one, each part complementing the other.

"I suppose there is nothing very profound about the above; it is seen throughout nature. We, as physicians, see it daily. For example, an older person who functions well on the outside, caring for himself or herself and managing a household, is brought into the hospital for perhaps a simple procedure. All the environmental stimuli with which he is familiar are removed, and suddenly the person is not able to function and relate to people, or to continue the usual level of intellectual activity.

"I suspect that this equation may be a common thread running through the lives of those whom you have described."

Yes, Robert Charman, it is.

That Mountain

AN EPILOGUE

*I*t seems significant that the conversations in this book were held during the days of diminishing light, late summer through fall and into winter; yet everyone with whom I talked was looking forward to something. Call it spring.

I keep thinking of others with whom I would like to talk. There is the librarian, now in a nursing home, but because the world of ideas has always been hers, it still is: introducing books to others, sharing thoughts, reading aloud, she knows no end to the richness abounding, and pays little heed to her physical limitation. I think of Old Fon, a woodsman in the North Country with more grandchildren than he can count, ninety now and frail, and alone, but cutting, splitting, stacking his three cords of wood every year, because "You have to be ready for the winter," he says. I think of the business man who lost count of time when he turned eighty, but who works tirelessly not only in his own garden but in other people's, because "It keeps you young to help things grow."

Leagues apart are the banker, the apple-grower, the music teacher and the others, but with them there is a concurrence. Each one saw clearly, not always easily and not always soon, what could be done with life; and each one recognized a Power to which life was linked. Jung made this plain when he wrote, "Among all my patients in the second half of life—that is to say over thirty-five—there has not been one whose problem in the last resort was not that of finding a religious outlook on life. It is safe to say that every one of them fell ill because he had lost that which the living religions of every age have given to their followers, and none of them has been really healed who did not regain his religious outlook."

Spring was at hand for me, not in longing or imagination but in reality, so I took off early one morning on a climb to hail the sun. The day was mine, as was the world of one small mountain. The ground was spongy in places where winter snow had lain long, the trees were still bare, but a swelling of buds soon to be leaves could be seen and there was in the air the fragrance of green growing things.

Before an hour had passed, I made my first halt near a spring. The water tasted no colder in April than it did in August, but if anything it was more delicious because I had not tasted it for so long. Periodic resting always makes me think of Icelandic ponies, so, with a cup of water held to my lips, I saluted them in memory and across the miles.

Years ago, when spending some time in Iceland, Bill and I had gone with a guide into the interior on the small horses. Everything we needed was in our saddle packs. Each day we rode deeper into that barren beautiful land, spending the nights at farmhouses along the way. We didn't have many words of Icelandic and our guide had fewer of English, but it took no words to understand one of the customs. On the first morning out from Reykjavik we had been riding for slightly less than an hour when our guide signaled to us to stop. He got off his horse, let the reins fall to the ground, threw himself down on the rich grass and closed his eyes. We did the same, but kept our eyes open. The three ponies grazed in as steady and deliberate a fashion as they did everything else. After five minutes we mounted and were on our way. This happened every hour throughout the day, sometimes by a stream where we could all drink; the time was longer at noon when we opened our lunch packets. The procedure surprised us at first, but we soon learned the reason for those frequent and regular stops. We were all refreshed.

Taking time out, even in the midst of events, reduces its urgency; and, curious as the act may seem, results in giving us more time rather than less. With the ponies, five minutes taken out of every hour was sufficient; with me, on my climb, time out was whenever there seemed good reason to pause—either for a view, or for reflection, or just to lie spread-eagled and feel at one with the Earth. Antaeus renewed his strength in just such a way.

Bill and I had climbed many mountains during the years we shared life, big ones in Switzerland, others in the British Isles and Iceland, some in the Rockies, and lesser ones in New England. Height had little to do with the sense of achievement, for the challenge was the same and the reward as thrilling. Before a climb, some time had always been spent in preparation. It might have been no more than to be sure boots were in good condition and the picnic lunch hearty enough; it might have meant securing ropes and pitons and the services of a local guide. Well do I remember the disappointment when, because of weather, plans had to be deferred to another day, or another week, or sometimes canceled altogether. That was true for Hekla in Iceland, for we never did get to the top because of the mists that persisted in shrouding it. But we learned that flexibility was as much a part of climbing equipment as a sound physique.

"Take care," were the words our Swiss guide said when we started up the Wildhorn, only he said them in French, "Prenez garde." It was a rule, perhaps the only rule; if disregarded, the consequences might have to be borne by others as well as oneself. Closely allied to care was watchfulness, not only for the loose rock but for the sudden opening of a view. Throwing off a rucksack and stretching out on turf or scree for a few moments was as gratifying as a meeting with other climbers and the exchange of words that ensued. The steeper the ascent and the thinner the air became, the more breathtaking was the view—not only of surrounding peaks and reaches of sky but downward into the valley. To see the way roads linked houses and villages and led on was to see a pattern emerge: there was a reason why things were as they were.

And no matter how steep it was, or difficult, we kept on going. It did not get easier. It called for more stamina as well as courage, but we never doubted that it would be worth it. Ahead, always ahead, was the summit. And the surprise. Meister Eckhart has put my feeling into words, "There is no stopping place in this life—no, nor was there ever for any man no matter how far along he had gone. Then, be ready at all times for the gifts of God, and always for new ones."

Note

During my conversations I took only a few notes because I did not want to impede the natural, easy flow of talk. Returning home, I wrote everything down immediately with all the fidelity and clarity that memory gave me. When each first draft was completed, it was sent to the person with whom I had talked. Often there were corrections to be made, and occasionally some changes were suggested; but what meant most to me was that something in the conversation had stimulated thinking, and usually more was added to an idea recorded in the typescript. Permissions were given to use specific quotations: the two poems of Elizabeth Coatsworth's and the prayer of Elizabeth Vining's. In each instance, these fitted so perfectly into the context that I felt they should be included.   E.Y.